Fabrizio Poli is CEO of Orville Aviation Consulting and partner in a number of other aviation ventures. He is also an accomplished Airline Transport Pilot having flown both private jets and for the airlines. Fabrizio is also a bestselling author and inspirational speaker and has been featured on TRT World, Russia Today (RT), Social Media Examiner, Bloomberg, Channel 5, Chicago Tribune, Daily Telegraph, City Wealth Magazine, Billionaire.com, Wealth X, Financial Times, El Financiero, Newsweek and many other Media offering insight on the aviation world. Fabrizio is also regularly featured as an Aviation Analyst on both Russia Today (RT) and TRT World show, Money Talks. Fabrizio is also a contributor to AvBuyer Magazine, where he shares his insights on the world of private aviation.

Fabrizio is also considered one of the world's top 30 experts in using LinkedIn for business. You can also follow Fabrizio's aviation videos on Biz Jet TV and/or tune into his weekly podcast, Quantum Action. Fabrizio is a 1st degree black belt in Taekwondo, keen yogi and golfer. He is married to Silvia and they have four children.

To book a complimentary one-to-one private jet strategy call, go to: www.orvilleaviation.com

To my children, Benjamin, Elrond, Nike and Kayla.

Fabrizio Poli

The Quantum Economy

How to Exponentially Dominate and Disrupt by Increasing Your Speed to Succeed

Austin Macauley Publishers
LONDON · CAMBRIDGE · NEW YORK · SHARJAH

Copyright © Fabrizio Poli 2023

The right of Fabrizio Poli to be identified as author of this work has been asserted by the author in accordance with sections 77 and 78 of the Copyright, Designs and Patents Act 1988.

All rights reserved. No part of this publication may be reproduced, stored in a retrieval system, or transmitted in any form or by any means, electronic, mechanical, photocopying, recording, or otherwise, without the prior permission of the publishers.

Any person who commits any unauthorised act in relation to this publication may be liable to criminal prosecution and civil claims for damages.

A CIP catalogue record for this title is available from the British Library.

ISBN 9781528933001 (Hardback)
ISBN 9781528967297 (ePub e-book)

www.austinmacauley.com

First Published 2023
Austin Macauley Publishers Ltd®
1 Canada Square
Canary Wharf
London
E14 5AA

Table of Contents

Reviews 13

Introduction 16

Part One: Market Trends, Technology and Amazing Global Opportunities 27

Chapter 1: Airports, Education and Prosperity 29

Singapore Airport 31

Education in Singapore 31

Helsinki Vantaa International Airport, Finland 32

The Finnish Schooling System 33

Vancouver International Airport, Canada 34

Canadian Schools 35

Connecting the Dots Between Airports, Schools and Prosperity 36

Airports of the Future 37

Quantum Economy Snippets 38

Chapter 2: America, Demographics and Technology 39

Business Trends for the Future 39

A Decentralised Economy Driven by Cryptocurrencies 41

Quantum Economy Snippets 43

Chapter 3: Where to Do Business   **45**

Asia Pacific   *45*

Singapore   *46*

Japan   *48*

Vietnam   *49*

North Korea   *50*

Africa   *54*

Montenegro: A Rising Hub for the Wealthy   *57*

Dominican Republic   *60*

Latin America   *64*

E-Commerce in Latin America   *68*

Quantum Economy Snippets   *69*

Part Two: Why the Biz Jet is the Ultimate Twenty-first Century Business Tool   **73**

Chapter 4: Who and Why Are People Using Private Jets?   **75**

Saving Employee Time   *76*

Increases Traveller Productivity, Safety and Security En-Route   *76*

Flying into Airports Where Scheduled Airlines Don't   *77*

Quantum Economy Snippets   *78*

Chapter 5: Is a Private Jet Safe?   **80**

When the Boss and/or Passenger Takes Over…   *83*

Core Facts   *84*

Monkeys Flying Biz Jets…   *84*

Quantum Economy Snippets   *86*

Chapter 6: Pilot Training and Selection   87

So Why Have There Been a Significant Increase in Business Jet Accidents?   92

The Parable of the Soccer Player   93

Should I Charter My Jet Out?   94

Quantum Economy Snippets   95

Chapter 7: Why Private Jet Travel Will Increase   96

1. The Internet is Driving More International Business   96

2. It is Easier to Start Businesses Today   97

3. The Wealthy are on the Increase   97

4. Airport Security   98

5. More Terrorism   99

6. Providing More Flexibility and Speed   100

Quantum Economy Snippets   102

Chapter 8: Should I Buy New or Pre-Owned   103

What Are the Chinese Up To?   104

Quantum Economy Snippets   106

Part Three: Business Cases for a Faster Future   107

Chapter 9: Wal-Mart, Tesco and Private Jets   109

Quantum Economy Snippets   113

Chapter 10: Does Flying by Biz Jet Increase Sports Performance?   114

Quantum Economy Snippets   118

Chapter 11: Where the Private Jet Can Allow Business, Your Hobby and Charity; All Work Together   120

Combining Business With Piloting	*123*
Charitable Flying	*124*
Quantum Economy Snippets	*124*

Chapter 12: Building a Restaurant Empire by Private Jet — **125**

His First Private Jet was a Key Milestone	*126*
Surviving to Thriving in the Covid Lockdowns	*126*
How it All Started	*128*
Tilman Buys a VVIP B767 for the Houston Rockets	*128*
Quantum Economy Snippets	*129*

Chapter 13: From High-School Drop-Out, to Entrepreneur, Fighter Jet Pilot, to Astronaut. Meet Jared Isaacman — **130**

Isaacman	*130*
Where It All Started	*130*
Jared's Aviator Path Begins	*131*
When Did Jared Start Flying Private?	*132*
Jared Starts a Private Air Force	*133*
Next Step, Space	*133*
When Conquering Space Helps Your Business on Earth…	*135*
Success is About Learning to Handle Fear	*136*
Quantum Economy Snippets	*136*

Chapter 14: Even Plumbers Can Fly By Private Jet — **137**

Introduced to Business Aviation	*138*
From Plumbing to the Music Industry	*139*

Quantum Economy Snippets	*140*
Chapter 15: Self-Development Gurus Go Private Jet	**142**
10X Your Business with a Private Jet	*145*
Mini-Van in the Sky	*148*
Quantum Economy Snippets	*149*
Chapter 16: Be Stupid, Buy a Jet:	**150**
A Lesson from a Billionaire	*150*
Quantum Economy Snippets	*152*
Chapter 17: Combining Flying as a Hobby with Business	**153**
Quantum Economy Snippets	*155*
Chapter 18: How Have Covid Lockdowns Influenced the Future of Business Travel?	**156**
Quantum Economy Snippets	*160*
Chapter 19: Maybe It's Time to Get a Custom Fit Private Jet	**161**
Quantum Economy Snippets	*163*
Chapter 20: The eVTOL Buzz	**164**
Quantum Economy Snippets	*166*
Chapter 21: Wrapping-Up to Speeding-Up	**167**
Quantum Economy Snippets	*170*

Reviews

"The best investment I've ever made was in myself, the second best was in my jet. I have doubled the size of my business in the last 12 months, by using my biz jet as a business tool. In this great book Fabrizio not only tells my story but explains in a very clear and distinct manner why a business jet will give you the edge in a world, where speed is becoming more and more the currency of the twenty-first century."

—Grant Cardone
Sales Training Expert and Best Selling author of *Be Obsessed or Be Average*, *The 10X Rule*, *Sell or Be Sold*, and *If You're Not First, You're Last*.

"Fabrizio has written a great book on a very interesting subject: time."

"In today's world a private jet is a key business tool, enabling you to multiply time. The benefits of reducing downtime between meetings, increasing your speed as you travel from one country to another and giving you a more effective balance between leisure and work, are all factors that increase business performance."

"When scaling your business on an international level, both in Europe and globally, effective time management is

paramount, in order to improve the quality of your life. This is why private jet travel trumps the airlines."

"For all entrepreneurs, taking their business to the next level, this is a must read!"

—Alfio Bardolla, Milan, Italy
CEO and Founder, Alfio Bardolla Training Group Spa (listed in Milan Stock Exchange) and bestselling author, '*Money Makes You Happy.*'

"This book is a masterpiece. Maybe the bible of the aviation industry and an insightful prognostic on where the industry is moving."

"The Quantum Economy" also shows how deep is Fabrizio's knowledge regarding business aviation operations, sales and customer experience.

"As for the man himself, Fabrizio is clearly one of the most enthusiastic and engaged professionals I have ever met. I've enjoyed learning from his vast knowledge of business particularly within the aviation sector and hope to do lots of business with him in the future."

"Kudos Fabrizio for an outstanding job."

—Ziad K. Abdelnour, New York, USA
President and CEO, Blackhawk Partners, Inc.
and Bestselling author, '*Economic Warfare*'

"An excellent overview of the changes taking place in the new economy. A must read."
—**Enzo Calamo, Vancouver, BC, Canada.**
CEO, Lugen Family Office

"Corporate jet travel is about more than convenience and comfort. It is THE way to more efficiently reach your customers and partners worldwide. As THE recognised thought leader in aviation travel, Fabrizio Poli again hits a homerun in dissecting the various factors to consider in choosing corporate jet travel, whether owning or leasing, in an entertaining and engaging way. A terrific follow-up to his book, 'Health 4 Flyers'!"
—**Jim Markland, Tampa, Florida, USA**
President—Hedge Fund Alternatives

Introduction

We are living in a world of accelerated change thanks to technology and innovation. As world renowned social media marketer, Gary Vaynerchuk puts it: *"Today your TV has become your radio and your phone your TV."* In the last 15 years we have seen new companies cause **major disruption** in the way we live and do business:

- Facebook started in 2004.
- YouTube started in 2005.
- Twitter started in 2006.
- Netflix started streaming in 2007.
- Apple launched the iPhone in 2007.
- Android phones in 2008.
- Airbnb started in 2008.
- Instagram started in 2008.
- Uber started in 2009.

In 1996, Kodak was the largest photo business in the world and turning over USD $16bn. In 2012, when they went bankrupt laying-off thousands of employees. Kodak was a linear organisation and was disrupted by exponential organisations. Peter Diamandis, Singularity University co-founder and creator of the X-prize, illustrates the difference between linear and exponential in many of his talks:

"If you were to take 30 linear steps, it would be one, two, three, four, five. After 30 linear steps you'd end up 30 paces or 30 meters away and all of us could pretty much point to where 30 paces away would be. But if I said to you take 30 exponential steps, one, two, four, eight, sixteen, thirty-two and said where would you end up? Very few people would say a billion meters away, which is twenty-six times around the planet."

Former head of innovation at Yahoo, Salim Ismail defines an **Exponential Organisation** as one whose impact (or output)-because of its use of networks or automation and/or its leveraging of the crowd is disproportionally large compared to its number of employees.

Kodak was the opposite having a large number of employees and lots of physical process and facilities.

In late 2010 two Stanford University grads, Kevin Systrom and Mike Krieger, founded Instagram to take on Kodak. Instagram is an exponential organisation taking advantage of high-resolution cameras in smart phones and the social media boom. Eighteen months later they already had 30 million users with just 13 employees. Facebook knocked on their door and Instagram was sold for USD $1bn!

In 2003, in a paper that introduced the term BRIC (Brazil, Russia, India and China) for the rising global players of the future, Jim O'Neill and his team at Goldman Sachs made some predictions about how quickly power and wealth would shift from West to East. They said that by 2008, China's GDP could be as high as USD $2.8 trillion; the fact of the matter is that it ended up more than USD $4.3 trillion. Brazil did even better by becoming two and a half times greater than projected. The increase in speed and acceleration is lifting billions of people out of poverty.

Those people, companies, institutions and nations that are worst placed to respond to acceleration will suffer more from its side effects, while those willing and capable of, will win in the market. Things like faster devices, or biological enhancements are things that will allow them to think better and act faster. The internet was dominated by people performing 'google searches' to find information. America-Vietnamese serial-entrepreneur Bill Nguyen declared; 'Google is dead.' What Nyugen means is that the web is moving away from an automated model pioneered by Google and towards the social approach favoured by Facebook, where your experience of the internet is filtered by that of your friends.

In 2016 we witnessed political disruption both in Europe with the UK voting to leave EU and Donald Trump winning the US election. In both cases mainstream media were telling a very different story than reality. Both games were won using social media. The internet is giving power to the people, with 'real people,' now communicating with 'real people.' Companies can now interact with each customer directly on social media and hear their opinions and adjust accordingly. Those that communicate and adjust the fastest are the ones that will win the business, speed is key in twenty-first century.

While the Internet has been extraordinary, it has only until recently connected the wealthiest. In 2010, 1.8 billion people were connected. Today, just over 2.8 billion are connected...

In other words, on a planet with a 7+ billion population, 4+ billion people are still not connected to the Internet. Three to 5 billion new consumers, who have never bought anything, never uploaded anything and never invented and sold anything, are about to come online and provide a mega-surge to the global economy. These people are not coming online like we did 20 years ago with a dial-up modem. They're coming online with a 1 Mbps connection and access to the world's information on Google, social media, cloud 3D printing, Amazon Web Services, artificial intelligence, crowdfunding, crowdsourcing and more.

Before COVID-19 pandemic hit the world, IATA (International Air Transport Association) was actually warning of an infrastructure crisis as it forecast a near doubling in demand for air travel over the next two decades. It said latest passenger forecast suggests around 7.2 billion air trips will take place in 2035, compared to 3.8 billion in 2016. However, an IATA-commissioned survey of recent travellers found that:

- 60% anticipate a return to travel within one to two months of containment of the COVID-19 pandemic but 40% indicate that they could wait six months or more.
- 69% indicated that they could delay a return to travel until their personal financial situation stabilises.

There are going to be less choices for passengers, as the number of airlines shrink and the number of frequencies operated reduce. Some city pairs, or routes, that have been operated with low frequency—say less than weekly—will perhaps be dropped altogether. Passengers will also opt for more direct routings to avoid having to pass through extra airports on layovers.

Ultra-High Net-worth Individuals (UHNWI) are defined as people with a net worth of over USD $30M. The world's UHNWI population—rose by 2.4% in the 12 months to January 2020, according to Knight Frank's Global Wealth Sizing Model. This places the total number of UHNWIs globally to more than 520,000 as of the end of 2020, with this number predicted to grow over next 10 years at a rate of 27%.

The Knight Frank Wealth Report still sees the US as the world's dominant wealth hub over their forecast period but Asia will see the fastest growth in UHNWIs over the next five years, at 39% compared with the 27% global average. By 2025, Asia will host 24% of all UHNWIs, up from 17% a decade earlier. The region is already home to more billionaires than any other (36% of the global total). The Chinese Mainland is the key to this phenomenon, with 246% forecast growth in very wealthy residents in the decade to 2025. The UHNW population is expected to rise to 663,483 by 2025.

According to business aviation intelligence company, JetnetIQ, there are 21,985 total business jets in the world, which equates to around 18,000 owners. If we divide the number of current UHNWIs worldwide by the number of private jets (18,000/520,000) we see that only 3.5% of them own a business jet.

Like after the 2001 9/11 terrorist attacks in the US, we saw the airline market shrink but private jet travel surge, as more of the wealthy turned to private jet ownership. My prediction is that the 3.5% will probably look more like a 15%. More about this later…

Rapid change is happening all over at a very fast pace and this is causing disruption, bringing down businesses like Blockbuster that for years had dominated the movie rental business. They were offered an opportunity to invest in Netflix and did not take it and now Netflix are dominating the movie business and growing, while Blockbuster is now part of the history books. In 2015, Amazon's Jeff Bezos had an estimated worth of around $34.8 billion, strong sales then increase by almost $25 billion 12 months later to propel him to richest person in the world at $90 billion in October 2017 and latest figure at time of writing in January 2022 shows him still sitting in the #3 spot at $177 billion, with Elon Musk #1 at $263 billion.

Bezos diversified his investments by acquiring the Washington Post newspaper, shares in space exploration company Blue Origin and health food store chain, Wholefoods. One of the key things Amazon did in 2016 was to increase Amazon Prime members, now making up more than half the online retailer's customer base, according to a new study. With most of the world in lockdown, during COVID-19, online sales have surged and consequently Amazon stock. Many that were reluctant to try online shopping have suddenly discovered how convenient and time saving it is.

Amazon has got FASTER and as a result is getting more valuable.

Fellow futurist, Jim Carroll, in his book: '*The Future Belongs to Those Who Are Fast*' talks about **three** important keys for success in business in the twenty-first century:

Transformation: What worked in the past surely won't work in the future! Everything is changing at a furious pace: business models, customers, products and services, new competitors, organisational structure.

Acceleration: Companies need to very quickly and continually reinvent themselves, particularly in terms of the products or services they offer, the markets they operate in, the business proposition at their core. In this world of IOE (**I**nternet **o**f **E**verything) global business models, speed is the key for future success.

Collaboration: In order to transform and accelerate, be relentless with structure. Constantly rethink the skills you employ, the partnerships you pursue and the insights you get from shared ideas. We're in the era of the global idea machine as witnessed with crowd-thinking and crowdfunding—align yourself to the new insight that comes from a connected organisation.

However, air travel has got slower…Since Concorde was retired in December 2003, supersonic civilian air travel has not yet returned. Terrorism has caused security in airports to increase but as a result our travel time takes longer with endless check-in lines, more flight delays and lots of lost baggage… So once we use the incredible technology we have been blessed with and connect with new people, opportunities and businesses around the world, how do we travel faster than the competition?

By biz jet, your exponential air travel tool.

- Not surprisingly biz jet activity worldwide has seen a 34-percent increase over the past five years and an estimated doubling of flight hours over the next 20 years, confirm that top companies increasingly realise the undeniable advantages provided by business aircraft.
- The number of biz jets used for business purposes is growing. In a 2019 report, using data from JETNET, NEXA Advisors reported that there were over 33,000 fixed-wing business aircraft around the world, with approximately 21,985 jets and 13,700 turboprops. The majority (nearly 21,000) were in North America, where the total number had increased on an annual basis by 2.4% (compounded) since 2004. As previously stated, only 3.5% of UHNWIs own their own private jet.
- Private Jets can fly into more than 5,000 U.S. public airports, while scheduled airlines serve just over 400 airports. The European fleet can fly to over 4.200 airports, with less than 350 serviced by the airlines.
- 2/3 of private jet flights are on routes not served by scheduled airlines.

However, worldwide the mainstream media have done a bad job by making the general public think that private jets are for the rich and famous, used by only large corporations and cost a lot of money. Being in the business of buying and selling private jets I have seen a need to tell the story differently because there are people out there using a biz jet as a real cutting-edge business tool. Interestingly companies that utilise business aircraft outperform non-business aviation users in several important financial measures, including annual earnings growth, stock and dividend growth, total share price, market capitalisation and other financial indicators.

As entrepreneurs and business owners how important thinking and acting fast is to survival in the twenty-first century? Speed is in an entrepreneur's DNA, moving quickly comes natural to them. Up until now it has been difficult to emphasise the importance of this in business but things are about to change...

In many situations business aviation is the best or only transportation option available, opening the door to global commerce for small-community and rural populations by linking them directly to population centres and manufacturing facilities. Studies have also shown that business aviation contributes greatly to local economies across the world. Biz jets allow employees to make a trip involving stops at several locations, then return to headquarters the same day. Hundreds or thousands of dollars can be saved on hotel rooms, rental cars, meals and other expenses that would be needed to make the same trip over several days via auto, train or airline transport.

Raymond "Ray" Kurzweil is an American author, computer scientist, inventor, futurist and co-founder of Singularity University. In a recent essay titled: The Law of Accelerating Returns, he stated: *"An analysis of the history of technology shows that technological change is exponential, contrary to the common-sense 'intuitive linear' view. So we won't experience 100 years of progress in the twenty-first century—it will be more like 20,000 years of progress (at today's rate).*

The 'returns,' such as chip speed and cost-effectiveness, also increase exponentially. There's even exponential growth in the rate of exponential growth. Within a few decades, machine intelligence will surpass human intelligence, leading to The Singularity—technological change so rapid and profound it represents a rupture in the fabric of human history. The implications include the merger of biological and non-biological intelligence, immortal software-based humans and ultra-high levels of intelligence that expand outward in the universe at the speed of light."

We are going to see more change in society; due to technology, in the next 25 years than in the previous 300.

In Richard Florida's book, '*Great Reset*' he talks about average transportation speeds and number of miles the average person will travel in their lifetime.

- **In the year, 1850**—Average speed 4 mph—Traveling 4 miles per day × 50 year life expectancy = 73,000 miles.
- **In the year, 1900**—Average speed 8 mph—Traveling 8 miles per day × 60 year life expectancy = 175,200 miles.
- **In the year, 1950**—Average speed 24 mph—Traveling 24 miles per day × 70 year life expectancy = 613,200 miles.

- **In the year, 2000**—Average speed 75 mph—Traveling 75 miles per day × 80 year life expectancy = 2,190,000 miles.
- **In the year, 2050**—Average speed 225–250 mph (projected)—Traveling 225 miles per day × 90 year life expectancy = 7,391,250 miles.

Over a 200-year period we are seeing humankind transitioning from a slow and difficult form of transportation to fast and painless. Going from 73,000 to 7.3 million is a 100X increase in human mobility and 4 mph speed to 225 mph is a 56.25X in speed increase. Now, think of the technological changes society has experienced just from 1850 to 2000…

The ultimate twenty-first century business tool is the biz jet, as it allows you to transform the way you travel, giving you more speed and becoming your exponential travel tool. This added speed will accelerate your business, opening more doors, allowing you to collaborate with more people and companies across the globe. The average speed of the human being between now and 2050 is going to increase to 225 mph and will travel 7.3 million miles, bringing you into the quantum economy.

Where are you going to go and what opportunities will this bring you?

Read on and hopefully this book will inspire you to move faster and to fascinating places, opening the doors to entrepreneurship in the twenty-first century…

Part One: Market Trends, Technology and Amazing Global Opportunities

Chapter 1
Airports, Education and Prosperity

"Teaching kids how to nourish their creativity and curiosity, while still providing a sound foundation in critical thinking, literacy and math, is the best way to prepare them for a future of increasingly rapid technological change."
—Peter H. Diamandis

An Aerotropolis is an urban plan in which the layout, infrastructure and economy is centred on an airport, existing as an airport city. It is similar in form and function to a traditional metropolis, which contains a central city core and its commuter-linked suburbs. The term was developed by academic and air commerce expert Dr John D. Kasarda in 2000, based on his prior research on airport-driven economic development.

Aerotropolis' are being developed all over the world and there is actually a correlation between education and airports, which consequently leads to prosperity. Below are two tables, one depicting the CNN Business Travellers 2016 Best

Airports and the other OECD ranking for Educational Systems for maths and science.

2016 Best airports for overall experience:

1. Changi International Airport (Singapore).
2. Incheon International Airport (Seoul, South Korea).
3. Haneda International Airport (Tokyo, Japan).
4. Taoyuan International Airport (Taipei, Taiwan).
5. Munich International Airport (Germany).
6. Kansai International Airport (Osaka, Japan).
7. Vancouver International Airport (Vancouver, Canada).
8. Helsinki International Airport (Vantaa, Finland).
9. Tallinn International Airport (Tallinn, Estonia).
10. Kloten International Airport (Zurich, Switzerland).

World Schooling Systems—Maths and Science Ranking

A 2015 study by the OECD ranked the Educational Systems by the results of kids aged 15 at Maths and Science. The ranking is very similar to the general ranking, with top tier Asian countries leading the list. Countries ranked on maths and science results for 15 year olds:

1. Singapore.
2. Hong Kong.
3. South Korea.
4. Japan.
5. Taiwan.
6. Finland.

7. Estonia.
8. Switzerland.
9. Netherlands.
10. Canada.

It very interesting to note that these two lists are almost identical. To prove the point, we will have a look at Singapore, Finland and Canada.

Singapore Airport

Singapore ranks both #1 for maths and science and wins all three titles for best airport for sleeping, best airport for layovers and best airport for overall experience. Singapore Changi Airport offers free and comfortable reclining loungers and massage chairs for passengers to recharge their batteries in between flights. This airport already has a butterfly garden, swimming pool and cinema.

With a current capacity of 66 million passengers a year, the opening of terminal four in 2017 will see this number rise to 82 million. Developers want Changi to eventually handle at least 130 million people a year.

A new Changi development containing an indoor forest with hiking trails and a 40-meter rain vortex falling from the roof is due to open in 2018.

Education in Singapore

In a short period of 50 years Singapore, a former British colony which started out as a low-cost, low-skill labour market, now boasts a highly skilled workforce where more than half are university graduates.

Literacy rates have skyrocketed, with Singaporean students amongst the best in the world when it comes to scoring at international exams.

OECD director for education Andreas Schleicher said its students have a good foundation in mathematics and science, which has contributed to Singapore's success and this is a factor coming into play with building such an awesome airport like Changi International.

Helsinki Vantaa International Airport, Finland

Helsinki Airport, owned by Finavia, has already been in the top class of airports for almost 20 years. The high world ranking is proof of the high level of the airport's operations and services.

Helsinki Airport is amongst the most popular transfer airports in Europe and is preparing to serve 20 million annual passengers by year 2020. The EUR 900-million development programme currently underway aims to preserve the strengths of Helsinki Airport. Short transfer times, friendly staff and world-class services will stay the same although passenger volumes increase.

In 2015, eight different surveys were carried out at Helsinki Airport. The data was gathered by organising surveys in the terminal, with in-depth interviews, mystery shopping and also with real-time data collection devices. Data is gathered on travel destinations and passenger types, among other things. Also, subjects such as the development of travel, passenger behaviour as well as needs and satisfaction at the airport were researched.

The surveys found passengers can be divided into four groups:

1. Those interested in experiences and pampering themselves (34%).
2. Passengers who appreciate quick and efficient service (26%).
3. Routine passengers (22%).
4. Passengers seeking a sense of safety who appreciate familiarity and clarity (18%).

It is important to note that 33% of the passengers of Helsinki Airport are frequent flyers. Finavia has been studying the commercial behaviour of passengers. This has revealed that there are great differences between nationalities. Typically, the largest purchases at the Helsinki Airport are carried out by Chinese and Russian passengers.

The Finnish Schooling System

Instead of control, competition, stress, standardised testing, screen-based schools and loosened teacher qualifications, Finnish schools are warm, collaborative, highly professionalised, with teacher-led encouragement and assessment.

Children in Finnish public schools are given not only basic subject instruction in math, language and science but learning-through-play-based preschools and kindergartens, training in second languages, arts, crafts, music, physical education, ethics and, amazingly, as many as four outdoor free-play breaks per day, each lasting 15 minutes between classes, no matter how cold or wet the weather is. Educators and parents in Finland believe that these breaks are a powerful engine of learning that improves almost all the "metrics" that matter most for children in school—executive function, concentration and cognitive focus, behaviour, well-being, attendance, physical health and yes, test scores, too. The homework load for children in Finland varies by teacher but is lighter overall than most other developed countries. This insight is supported by research, which has found little academic benefit in childhood for any more than brief sessions of homework until around high school.

Vancouver International Airport, Canada

Vancouver Airport has a decent increase in passenger numbers each year and is planning to improve its passenger volume even further. But to achieve that, the airport has to attract more flights. One way they are achieving that is by reducing airplane ground times. How long an airplane spends on the ground dictates the cost to that airline. If an airport can decrease that time, the airline is happy because it pays fewer fees. And the airport is happy because it can soon welcome another airplane at the same gate, which means more passengers moving through the terminal. But reducing this time is no easy task for an airport. In order to attract more passengers Vancouver Airport is focusing on a wide range of small improvements to increase customer satisfaction, including:

- Better washrooms—touch-free, fully accessible, vibrant and modernised amenities and with ample space to navigate even with all that carry-on.
- Constantly evolving dining and shopping opportunities.
- A layout that, despite the airport's size, makes everything feel close.
- More free Wi-Fi, laptop and phone charging areas and TV viewing areas.
- New play areas for kids.
- Softer seating among carefully placed plants and art boxes in gate areas.
- Way-finding that creates an intuitive path for all the different passenger flows within the terminal.

Canadian Schools

The Canadian schooling system ranks #10 in the world because teachers, teacher unions, school boards, the government—work together for the benefit of the students. There is also a required rigorous training for teachers—not just before you can become a teacher but throughout their entire career.

Canada, has developed a teacher training program tailored for undergraduates who know they want to be a teacher once they graduate but also teacher colleges where you go for either a year or two of training, depending upon which Canadian province you live in, that Canadians must attend before they become a teacher.

Making sure that teachers are well-prepared to face the challenges is a key success factor. But it's not just training teachers that makes the Canadian school system one of the best; it's also because of how they train them. The country's system is so successful because they have been able to reduce the impact of socioeconomic status in their students' education and they tailor their teaching to meet the needs of their diverse student population and communities. Every school in Canada staffs a full-time "student success teacher," who devotes his or her time to the students who need it most. This helps each student discover and develop their talents. Focusing on the one is producing a more capable and confident work force. Education is typically seen as the most powerful route to improving private and public prosperity and well-being.

Connecting the Dots Between Airports, Schools and Prosperity

Educated people not only earn higher incomes but also contribute disproportionally to business innovation, productivity and national economic performance. There is a strong and direct relationship between educational attainment and economic growth and we can clearly see this in the correlation between successful schooling systems and best airports.

Education also affects social outcomes. Higher educational attainment has been linked to increased civic engagement, higher life satisfaction and lower crime rates. There is also strong evidence proving more educated people make decisions that lead to healthier and longer lives. Education is an important contributor to well-being and a critical force for driving success.

There is a clear connection between education, airport development that consequently influences the economy. In a world where technology is accelerating more and more and thanks to social media connecting people around the world has not only become easier but also a lot faster, the next step is getting on a plane. We have already seen that the internet has brought a massive increase in air travel and as I stated previously in this book by 2035 air travel will have doubled as most of the planet get online and connect.

Airports of the Future

I laugh when I read about building a new runway at London Heathrow or Vancouver Airports because by the time these are completed the technology of aircraft will be very different and therefore create the need for a different type of airport infrastructure.

Most short to medium distance air travel, by 2030, will happen via Vertical Take-Off and Landing (VTOL) and electric flying machines or via ground transport hyper-loop.

With Elon Musk's Space X intending to land cargo on Mars five years from now—this technology could very well end up being used on earth for faster terrestrial flights. Basically, Musk's idea is to fly groups of 100 people in a rocket from any two points on the globe in less than an hour.

Flying at a maximum speed of 27,000 km/hr (17,000 mph), a hypersonic trip from New York to Shanghai in Musk's proposed craft would take 39 minutes, down from the current nonstop time of about 15 hours. Los Angeles to Toronto would take just 24 minutes. London to Dubai in a mere 29 minutes.

Cities like Vancouver would create a high-speed ferry to shuttle passengers to an offshore barge where the rocket launches.

Quantum Economy Snippets

- ➢ Aerotropolis urban plan in which the layout, infrastructure and economy is centred on an airport, existing as an airport city.
- ➢ Clear connection between education, Aerotropolis and economic development.
- ➢ Air travel to double by 2035, +7 billion people connected via the internet and social media.
- ➢ The Airports of the future will have to cater for VTOL electric vehicles and rockets, carrying people from one point of the globe to another in less than an hour.

Chapter 2
America, Demographics and Technology

"I learned how to become wealthy because I asked the right questions when I was broke."

—**Mark Cuban**

Business Trends for the Future

If you search the airlines with the worst safety records you will find that 90% come from countries in emerging markets. So, what can you do if you have the need to fly to these places?

You know the answer to that question…let's look at trends and places of the present and future where to do business.

The major economical disruptions of the future will be driven by demographics and technology. Developing countries will grow nearly 7 times faster than developed countries. Developing countries will grow by 24%, while developed countries will grow by only 3.6% between 2010 and 2030. More than 20 of the world's top 50 cities ranked by GDP will be located in Asia by the year 2050, up from 8 in

2007. More than half of Europe's top 50 cities will drop off the list, as will 3 in North America.

Technology diffusion will continue and even speed up by 2030. The number of mobile-only internet users is still only 14 million today but expected to grow 34% p.a. by 2030, connecting 60% of the world's population to mobile broadband.

Technological progress increased 40% to 60% faster in developing countries then in developed countries between 1990s and 2000s.

The technology gap between the developed and developing countries will narrow. People have moved from the countryside to cities for millennia but never have cities grown at the speed and scale they are today. In 2010, for the first time in history, more than half of the world's population lived in cities. Cities account for over 80% of global GDP.

According to the UN, an extra 2.4 billion people will live in cities by 2050, bringing the global sum of city dwellers to 6.3 billion—67% of the world's population.

Nearly 94% of those who move to cities in the next few decades will come from the developing world. The emerging-market middle class will double its share of global consumption (from a third to two-thirds) by 2050.

New technology is morphing these dwellings into 'smart cities' creating huge business opportunities with a market value of USD $1.5 Trillion in 2020.

Ageing will also be a key trend in global demographics. By 2050, one in every five people will be at least 60 years old. The overall ratio of old to young is set to almost double from current levels.

Automation and globalisation have shifted a lot of manufacturing (and the jobs related to it) to developing countries. This is now happening with office jobs in many services industries. Cities remain best placed to take advantage of technological change, whether incremental or disruptive, which allows them to access global markets, discover new opportunities in education and training, improve healthcare, store and use big data and much else besides.

We have already discussed the high number of airports in both the US and Europe. There are emerging economies that bring entrepreneurial opportunities in areas of the world with limited commercial routing and low volume of connections, it is significantly easier and more efficient to travel private jet to and from these locations. Again, speed is key with more opportunities being grasped by the fastest.

A Decentralised Economy Driven by Cryptocurrencies

The benefits of cryptocurrencies are many. One of the advantages being the fact these currencies, by their nature, are secured and are easy to transact. Another key advantage is you can make a payment in a cryptocurrency 24/7, any day of the year. You are probably thinking you can do that with a credit card, you can but there are limits. With crypto you can buy a $15M villa on a Sunday afternoon, when the banks are shut.

A cryptocurrency transaction also cuts out the middleman such as the credit card company and/or a bank with processing time being just a few minutes.

Cryptocurrencies will be very beneficial in the area of real estate. This is because bitcoin, one of the leading cryptocurrencies, is powered by blockchain. The blockchain is a decentralised ledger that allows users to transact with each other directly and the biggest benefit of a blockchain is that a transaction can never be reversed. Thus, the chances of fraud get minimised. In the case of real estate, in most developing countries, land records are in a mess. Tracking these records is not easy. Often these records are tampered. Once these records go on a blockchain it will not be easy to tamper the records and this could ideally solve a major problem for people who have most of their wealth in real estate. Poor people with no land records can be benefited through the use of cryptocurrency.

There can be no identity theft in a cryptocurrency transaction. The person who wants to send cryptocurrencies is in total control of their transaction as compared to a credit card transaction, where the third party bank is in control of the transaction.

Cryptocurrencies are truly global and are not bound by the boundaries of any country. Thus, transactions become very easy. Secondly, there is no third party that can block your account in case the account has been misused. In the case of cryptocurrencies, the owner owns the private key and thus no third party can take away your money, unless you lose the private key.

Cryptocurrencies allow you the ultimate ownership of your own money. Thus, while people are worried that digitalisation will allow the governments to take control of your bank account, the scope of such a thing happening with cryptocurrencies is limited because the entire operation is decentralised.

With the advent of the internet, social media and now cryptocurrencies we are seeing the decentralisation of the economy on a global scale. This is putting the power into the hands of the entrepreneur like never before in the history of this planet. This decentralised economy is going to be opening opportunities in many parts of the globe, where speed will be the determining factor between the winners and the losers.

Quantum Economy Snippets

- With US corporate tax rate lowered to 21% coupled with a reduction on regulations by 75%, America's economy will be on an upward surge.
- 90% of aircraft accidents happen to airlines from emerging nations. Another good reason to fly in and out there with your own jet.
- The major disruptions in the future economy will be coming from demographics and technology.
- Developing nations are growing 7X faster than developed countries.
- More than 20/50 of top 50 cities ranked by GDP will be located in Asia.
- Number of mobile internet users will be growing 34% p.a. by 2030.
- Technology gap between developed and developing nations will narrow.
- By 2050, 67% world's population will live in cities.
- By 2050, 20% world's population will be over 60 years old.

- The best business opportunities of the future lie in the emerging nation economies and getting in and out fast is key, hence the increased need for private jet travel.
- A decentralised economy driven by cryptocurrencies.

Chapter 3
Where to Do Business

"Time is more valuable than money. You can get more money, but you cannot get more time."

—Jim Rohn

Asia Pacific

With developing economies accounting for 66% of all new wealth creation, while the US and Europe is only 33%. Just over 60% of these new millionaires are coming from the Asia-Pacific region.

With Asia-Pacific producing four times more billionaires than the Americas during 2015 and leading all regional groups in terms of growth rate of billionaire population and wealth, at 14.1% and 16.5% respectively. Asia leads all regions in growth of both billionaire population and wealth at 15.2% and 19.6% respectively. Asia was also responsible for 57% of all net billionaire additions and 70% of all new billionaire wealth in 2015.

Global growth overall grew by 11.9%. Asia-Pacific, excluding Japan is the fastest growing region with China and

India accounting for 25% and 44% of the growth, respectively.

Technological innovation and wealth go hand in hand. The Asia-Pacific region is becoming the centre of wealth and has unprecedented access to technology. This plays right into the hands of Fintech companies who are springing up in China and the rest of region using the preferred tools of their rich new client base to give them low cost, transparent access to the capital markets.

Rather than talk about China and India, which we all know are great places to go to do business, I'd like to talk about a few places that aren't so obvious.

Singapore

We have already talked about both Singapore's main airport and their thriving schooling system as being ranked #1 in the world. Not surprisingly, biz jet activity is on the increase in and out of Singapore, as it has positioned itself as one of the wealth capitals of the world. It is home to the Singapore Freeport, the world's largest high-security storage facility for art and high value collectible items started operations in May 2010; with leading arts business Christie's establishing its Fine Art Storage Services within the Freeport facility to provide storage services to its global clientele. Another top auction house, Spink, has chosen Singapore as its base to tap into Asia's growing market for coins, stamps, medals and banknotes collectibles.

Art businesses setting up in Singapore will also benefit from the other exciting developments in the Singapore arts scene. The inaugural Art Stage Singapore in January 2011, will be the latest art fair by the former Director of Art Basel, Lorenzo Rudolf, that will position Singapore as the arts hub for the Asia-Pacific.

Singapore has also launched a USD $330M National Robotics Programme (NRP) to drive and coordinate robotics technology research, solutions development and adoption across the public and private sectors.

The goal is to develop differentiating enabling technology research capabilities.

Singapore is playing a lead demand role in driving the development of innovative solutions in select sectors. They are initially focusing on accelerating the development of innovative solutions for the manufacturing, logistics, healthcare, transport, environmental services and security industries.

Singapore also has another airport, Seletar Airport and it is purely dedicated to business aviation. Flying in and out of Seletar Airport does not require slots, offering users the flexibility to plan their flights to best suit their needs.

In Singapore, business aviation has been growing steadily at a compounded annual growth rate (CAGR) of 2.1% since 2011.

Developing a strong service model to enhance Singapore as a destination for high net-worth individuals and multinational companies, Seletar Airport has the unique offering of an uncongested secondary airport with greater privacy, flexibility and convenience.

Capable of supporting business jet operations to the class of Bombardier Global Express XRS, Dassault Falcon 7X or Gulfstream GV, Seletar Airport is well positioned to tap on Asia's strong growth momentum.

Japan

Japan has one of the most complex demographic challenges, fuelled by a population that is quickly both aging and shrinking. With 127 million people and a birth-rate of 1.39 children per woman, the country's overall population will drastically fall to less than 87 million by 2060; a full 40% of those 87 million will be 65 or older. This will bring Japan to a 40% reduction to its overall working-age population between 2000 and 2050.

This is scary but the Japanese people being both resilient and innovative, see opportunity in all this. Japanese tech companies are already at the forefront of creating solutions to help their aging-shrinking population. One good example The Japanese company Cyberdyne, is building powered exoskeletons designed to assist the elderly at work and at home. Toyota has begun testing "human support robots" that can move around rooms and pick up objects. Panasonic is currently working on a bed that transforms into a wheelchair. These new, innovative technologies will be exported to other countries creating more opportunities to do business internationally. Over the past decade.

Japanese officials have been moving toward making the island nation more welcoming to business aircraft operators. The results have been slow but steady, with business aviation movements in Japan rising 2.2% annually from 2010 through 2014 and international business aviation movements increasing at an annual rate of 3.3% during the same period.

Vietnam

Vietnam today is made up of 93.5 million people with average age of 30.3 years old—is defined by a growing population of young coders, engineers, entrepreneurs and students driving economic growth and technological innovation. According to PricewaterhouseCoopers, Vietnam could be the fastest growing of the emerging economies by 2025, with a potential growth rate of almost 10% per annum in real dollar terms. This could push it up to around 70% of the size of the UK economy by 2050.

The World Bank has described the transformation of the Vietnamese economy over the last 25 years as "remarkable," with economic and political reforms translating into higher incomes. Vietnam is expected to see its ultra-wealthy population rise by 170% to 540 over the next decade—the highest rate of growth in the world. Vietnamese millionaire numbers are expected to be boosted by strong growth in the local healthcare, manufacturing and financial services sectors.

As a result of several land reform measures, Vietnam has become the world's largest producer of cashew nuts, with a one-third global share; the biggest producer of black pepper, accounting for one-third of the world's market; and the second largest rice exporter after Thailand. It also has the highest percentage of land use for permanent crops—6.93%—of any nation in the Greater Mekong Sub-region. Vietnam is now one of Asia's most open economies: two-way trade is around 160% of GDP, more than twice the ratio for China and over four times that of India. Besides rice, key exports are coffee, tea, rubber and fishery products, with key trading partners including China, Japan, Australia, ASEAN countries, the US and Western Europe.

Vietnam is also going through a tech boom that is truly driving the economy. Vietnam barely had any IT companies 15 years ago but now there are close to 14,000 IT businesses spanning hardware, software and digital content. The Vietnamese government sees the tech sector as the linchpin of the country's economic growth, according to Mr Long Lam, CEO of Quang Trung Software City (QTSC), Vietnam's largest software park. It has heavily invested in infrastructure and passed economic policies encouraging both domestic and international entrepreneurs to start businesses.

Vietnam currently has 20 civil airports, including seven international airports (Noi Bai, TanSon Nhat, Cat Bi, Phu Bai, Da Nang, Chu Lai and Can Tho) and 13 local airports. Of these, only Noi Bai and Tan Son Nhat operate frequent international flights. The airport and airline infrastructure are currently growing.

Ho Chi Minh's Tan Son Nhat Airport has an FBO (**Fi**xed **B**ased **O**peration, basically a private jet terminal) managed by Vector Aviation. The FBO recorded 162,349 aircraft movements in its first year (2011) and activity is continuously growing.

North Korea

US President Donald Trump and North Korean leader, Kim Jong-un, meetings can potentially open some incredible new opportunities, we just have to see how the new administration deals with this relationship. Infrastructure and mining present the first points of interest, according to investment mogul Mark Mobius.

For Mobius, the long-time executive chairman of Templeton Emerging Markets Group and founder of Mobius Capital Partners, who pointed to North Korea's population of 25 million as remarkable opportunities for investors adding to South Korea's market of 50 million.

In a recent interview with CNBC Squawk Box Europe Mobius said, *"That means a much bigger market and to me the most exciting thing is the opportunity to have a bridge between South Korea, China and Russia. Because then you would be able to have railroads and roads going north through North Korea into these huge nations, a tremendous opportunity."*

Some investors have previously made note of North Korea's large, disciplined and relatively cheap workforce, however, have questioned the ability of the population to catch up with a modern economy, because of the country being closed off from much of the rest of the world until recently. Mobius was confident in the potential of the labour force.

"The North would be able to catch up very, very quickly, because the educational background is pretty good in the North and let's face it, look what they developed—nuclear capability is a technological feat with amazing proportions," Mobius said. *"So I believe they would catch up very quickly and the South would help them do that."*

South Korea has already offered concessions of aid and trade as part of potential peace deals.

North Korea has 78 usable airfields and their national airline, Air Koryo, joined IATA in late 1990s. North Korea has proclaimed a program to upgrade several airports to international standards. However, apart from Pyongyang Sunan International Airport and a few that receive irregular service by Air Koryo, commercial aviation in North Korea is practically non-existent and most airfields appear to be military use. However, as the economy opens-up and can see the airports opening to receive private jets, carrying entrepreneurs ready to do new deals.

Besides the workforce, North Korea has trillions of dollars' worth of natural resources—North Korea Resources Institute in Seoul estimated in 2013 that the country's mineral reserves could be worth $6 trillion.

Mobius—who has been operating in emerging and frontier markets for more than three decades, is very bullish on the opportunities in North Korea.

Mobius further elaborated on this: "We look at it first in terms of the mining capability—rare earths, oil, gas, there are tremendous resources in the North that could be exploited," he said. "Then of course the consumption revolution will take place once the standard of living begins to move up. So I'd say in the beginning it would be the resources and the transport—railroads, roads, going up north through to China and to Russia."

President Trump even suggested building some hotels on North Korea's lovely beaches, to lure in tourists and boost the economy.

Japanese newspapers reported that North Korean leader, Kim Jong-un, lived and was educated near Bern in Switzerland. Reports alleged that he attended the private English-language International School of Bern in Gümligen under the name 'Chol-pak' or 'Pak-chol' from 1993 to 1998.

At school, it's claimed he was a fan of basketball and was chaperoned the entire time by a bodyguard. Subsequently it was reported that Kim Jong-un attended the Liebefeld Steinhölzli state school in Köniz under the name 'Pak-un' or 'Un-pak' from 1998 until 2000 as the son of an employee of the North Korean embassy in Bern. This was partly confirmed by the Köniz authorities. Classmates who knew Mr Kim have recalled he had a good sense of humour and loved winning but did not like to discuss politics. If it's true that Mr Kim went to an English-language school, we know he is at least proficient in English. In addition, it's been claimed he had an obsession with American basketball players like Michael Jordan during his youth, so it's likely he picked up some English that way.

At the start of the meeting with US President Donald Trump on 12 June 2018, it seemed that Mr Kim was able to speak English well. He greeted Trump by saying: 'Nice to meet you, Mr President.' However, he used an interpreter throughout the rest of the meeting.

Mr Kim's friendship with former NBA star Dennis Rodham started in 2013 when Rodman made his first trip to North Korea with Vice Media correspondent Ryan Duffy, to host basketball exhibitions.

He met Kim Jong-un there and later declared him, "a friend for life."

Rodman told Good Morning Britain: "I hang out with him all the time. We laugh, we sing karaoke, we do a lot of cool things together like skiing and riding horses."

This friendship would indicate Mr Kim's openness to western culture and investment.

As always it will be those that travel by private jet to North Korea that pick up the most lucrative deals. Like in every new industry, the early birds are the ones that make the big bucks.

Africa

By 2050 the UN predicts there will be 2.5 billion Africans, about a quarter of the global population. And 10 of the youngest countries in the world will be on the continent. Interestingly, from 2000 to 2013, the number of millionaires on the continent grew by more than 145%, compared to the worldwide growth rate of 73%.

In recent years, most of the 'new millionaires' have been young entrepreneurs and investors who have created promising businesses and invested in lucrative sectors of Africa's fast-growing economies.

In recent years, most of the 'new millionaires' have been young entrepreneurs and investors who have created promising businesses and invested in lucrative sectors of Africa's fast-growing economies. Africa has been getting a lot of attention lately in the fashion world and for good reason. From Nigeria to South Africa and everywhere in between, new and fresh talent is entering the international style game with something totally unique. And it's not just the amazing designs inspired by the colours, sounds and heritage of the continent that have captured the attention of some of the biggest players in the industry. African designers are doing fashion on their own terms by putting local resources, artisanal skills and sustainable production at the forefront of their business models. While current fashion might be dominated by American and European designers and brands, the future looks very much like coming from Africa.

In the long term, three powerful positive trends are likely to sustain Africa's growth.

1. Africa has a young population with a growing labour force—a highly valuable asset in an ageing world. In 2034, Africa is expected to have the world's largest working-age population of 1.1 billion. In recent times, it has had some success in creating jobs—21 million new stable (formal, wage paying) jobs over the past five years and 53 million over the past 15. Stable jobs grew at a rate of 3.8% between 2000 and 2015, 1% faster than growth in the labour force.
2. Africa is still urbanising and much of the economic benefit lies ahead. Productivity in cities is three times as high as in rural areas and, over the next decade, an additional 187 million Africans will live in cities, according to the United Nations. This urban expansion is contributing to rapid growth in consumption by households and businesses. Household consumption grew at a 4.2% compound annual rate between 2010 and 2015—faster than the continent's GDP growth rate—to reach $1.3 trillion in 2015. It is projected that Africa's consumers will spend $2 trillion by 2025.

   Nigerian consumers alone may account for up to 30% of Africa's consumption growth over the next decade. Other segments to target include households earning more than $20,000 per annum in South Africa and Morocco, two of Africa's most diversified economies with a large consumer base, or those earning $5,000 to $20,000 in some of the fast-growing economies of East and West Africa.

3. African economies are also well positioned to benefit from rapidly accelerating technological change that can make growth easier. East Africa is already a global leader in mobile payments. Smart phones are expected to be in the hands of 50% of the population by 2020 from only 2% in 2010.

In Sub-Saharan Africa, cellular-enabled machine-to-machine connections are expected to grow by around 25% per annum to 30 million by 2020, according to GSMA Intelligence, changing the game in sectors from healthcare to power.

One of the biggest challenges doing business on the African continent is the lack of transport infrastructure, such as railroads, roads and airports.

Flying private jet inevitably, is always the best way to travel, in particular in this region of the world. The airline networks are not as developed as those in North America and Europe. According to a Bombardier forecast, there are currently 350 large business jets operating in Africa and that figure is projected to grow to 960 by 2020. Operations in Africa are focused primarily on the main centres of commerce and industry, with South Africa, Morocco and Nigeria being the leading centres. North Africa is experiencing, significant growth while the market is also expanding in the sub-Saharan region, with considerable growth in countries such as Angola,

Democratic Republic of Congo, Mozambique and Tanzania.

Montenegro: A Rising Hub for the Wealthy

In 2007, CNB journalist Robert Frank published a book called *"Richistan."* He noticed the wealth-community was growing and increasingly becoming a self-contained world, with its own health-care system (concierge doctors), travel system (private jets, destination clubs) and language. ("Who's your household manager?"). These people also did not live in one location but moved about a lot. They had created their own breakaway republic one Robert Frank called, Richistan. The people from Richistan tend to gather in certain upcoming areas of the world, as well as doing business in London, New York and Singapore.

One new upcoming place they are starting to flock to is Tivat in Montenegro. Montenegro is in the south of the Adriatic and unique in many ways. With much natural wealth, beauty, mild beaches, clear lakes, fast rivers and gorgeous mountains in such a compact area as in Montenegro. In the morning you can wake up along the beautiful Adriatic coast, have lunch on the banks of Skadar Lake and enjoy an evening walk in the Montenegrino mountains. Montenegro cannot leave you indifferent.

Montenegro is rapidly becoming an alternative European hub to Montecarlo, for HNWIs and UHNWIs. Tivat's Porto Montenegro was conceived and developed by Canadian entrepreneur Peter Munk, founder of Barrick.

Gold—the world's largest listed mining company—who, with an international group of investors led by Lord

Rothschild, envisioned and financed the transformation of a derelict naval base into a major yachting destination. In only 10 years, Porto Montenegro has established itself as a prime destination for the yachting community. Also geographically well positioned for those wanting to sail to the Greek islands, Porto Montenegro is an ideal location where to park your super yacht.

Recently, the Investment Corporation of Dubai (ICD), the principal investment arm of the government of Dubai, acquired Porto Montenegro Marina and Resort from Montport Capital. The acquisition is said to be in alignment with ICD's strategy to add high quality international assets in fast growing markets to its substantial portfolio. The transaction marks ICD's first investment in Montenegro and the yacht marina sector, both of which are expected to experience strong growth in coming years.

Montenegrin Prime Minister Milo Djukanovic says the government will continue to work closely with the new investors to implement a clear nautical tourism development strategy in Tivat and Boka Bay and to further position Montenegro as a high-end tourist destination.

In addition to 450 yacht parking bays already built and fully occupied and with the necessary approvals in hand to build another 400 berths plus develop land with a BUA of 280,000sq m, the resort has the potential to double in size and become the leading luxury yacht port on the Mediterranean.

"Looking ahead, our aim is to realise Porto Montenegro Marina and Resort's full long-term potential," says Al Shaibani. "Our priority at ICD is to support management in the fulfilment of its ambitious plans and to further establish Montenegro as a prime European yachting destination."

The construction of Montenegro's Tivat Airport's new multi million Euros terminal is underway. The expansion project includes the construction of a new 13.000 square metre terminal to the north of the existing facility, as well as the extension of the manoeuvring area and the rehabilitation and extension of the runway in order to achieve compliance with the International Civil Aviation Organisation's (ICAO) safety standards. Tivat Airport's capacity is already insufficient to handle the high demand during the peak summer months. It has been identified as a barrier to growth of the country's tourism industry by limiting the access of international tourists to Montenegro. The project will address this issue by increasing handling capacity of the passenger terminal to three million travellers per year and adding a further nine aircraft stands that will provide sufficient capacity for the next ten years and improve service quality. The project also entails catering for business aviation, as many of the super yacht owners are also jet owners.

Montenegro is also attracting a lot of attention as it is very rapidly becoming one of the best places to do business in Europe. Starting a company in Montenegro takes on average about a week and requires no start-up capital. With corporate taxes at 9% and both royalties and capital gains at that number too this is attracting a lot of new entrepreneurs and already established wealthy.

Montenegro also offers relief from taxes on foreign source income under an extensive network of tax treaties, although the United Kingdom and most European countries dominate the list it does include South Korea, China, India, Malaysia and some African countries.

Dominican Republic

According to the US State Department, the Dominican Republic has the largest economy in the Caribbean and Central American region and is the seventh largest economy in Latin America. Over the last 25 years, the Dominican Republic has had the fastest-growing economy in the Western Hemisphere—with an average real GDP growth rate of 5.3% between 1992 and 2018. Recent growth has been driven by construction, manufacturing, tourism and mining.

The country is the site of the third largest gold mine in the world, the Pueblo Viejo mine. Thanks to geological profile of the country, it is currently catalogued as the second largest gold deposit in America and also produces a wide range of mineral resources such as: silver, bauxite, ferronickel, clay, industrial minerals, larimar, amber, slabs, limestone, gypsum, salt, among other metallic resources. This sector presents a high participation of Foreign Direct Investment (FDI), thanks to the increase in the production levels of gold, marble and the main aggregate materials for construction.

The Dominican Republic is the most visited destination the Caribbean. The year-round golf courses are major attractions. A geographically diverse nation, the Dominican Republic is home to both the Caribbean's tallest mountain peak, Pico Duarte and the Caribbean's largest lake and lowest point, Lake Enriquillo. The island has an average temperature of 26°C (78.8°F) and great climatic and biological diversity. It is one of the favourite destinations for American and European tourists, due to its beautiful landscapes and the high quality of its hotel offer. The nation has more than 70,000 rooms that host about seven million tourists annually, which places this sector as one of the most important in the

Dominican economy, as it is the largest source of wealth and foreign exchange in the country.

This segment has a competitive hotel offer, a trained workforce, a modern infrastructure and a legal and institutional framework that encourages investment in this sector. For this reason, the country stands out as the most attractive tourist destination and golf course in the Caribbean for foreign investment.

The Dominican Republic has fertile soils and lands suitable for growing fruits and vegetables all year round, making it one of the most important sectors of its economy, which according to government data during the year contributed US$3,645.15 million to national production, equivalent to 4.1% of total GDP. The livestock, forestry and fishing sectors have also had an interesting growth of 3.5%.

Among the most productive crops are sugar, rice, coffee, cocoa and bananas, which are mainly exported to the United States, Haiti, Canada and India.

The Dominican Republic has favourable climatic conditions, ideal for attracting private investment in various energy projects in the country. For example, in the field of wind energy, its coastal regions in the southwest and north of the country have the potential to produce 30,000 MW. In the field of solar photovoltaic energy, thanks to its geographical position in the Caribbean, it has high levels of solar radiation throughout the year and this gives it a generation capacity of 50,000 MW.

Former US Treasurer Rosario Marín and the executive president of the World Travel and Tourism Council (WTTC), Julia Simpson, recognise the Dominican Republic's potential to attract tourists who after the pandemic are looking for a greater connection with nature.

Simpson says that the Dominican Republic is doing the job of preserving the environment because it understands that is what it has to offer to tourists or those looking to connect with nature.

She points out that it is throughout the region that the dynamism of that sector is coming back.

"It is coming back, it is coming back because people are looking for nature and also in Europe and the United States, for example, they have money, they have their savings, they have not been able to spend or enjoy traveling. So they are so eager to get out and come to Latin America."

While referring to the preservation of the environment in Quisqueya, the world leader of the private sector in tourism and travel emphasises that, "yes, it is doing the job, right, right, what happens in your country, which is very important, is that you recognise that you have to protect nature, because it is your product, not that I want to justify the word product with nature but it is what you have to offer, then people are looking for that. Also connecting with communities and getting to know other communities."

Jorge Hazoury and his family are the owners of Cap Cana, today's premier destination for the world's elite, over 6,200 acres includes more than three miles of powder-like sand beaches, a protected harbour marina only minutes away from one of the best fisheries of the world, the Punta Espada Golf Course, an award winning golf course designed by Jack Nicklaus; school district with the Cap Cana Heritage School, a bilingual school accredited by Advanced, providing neoteric education from Early Childhood through 12th grade and the

UNIBE University Cap Cana Campus, that offers complete and innovative programs for all levels of university degrees. This destination has also first class spas, five star hotels such as the Relais and Chateaux Eden Roc at Cap Cana hotel, the Sanctuary Cap Cana, The Secrets Cap Cana Resorts and soon to come the Hyatt Ziva and Zilara. Over 30 restaurants including four diamond awarded AAA restaurants, fitness centres, convention centres and an Adventure park.

The Stables, equestrian City, the biggest and most complete equestrian centre in the Caribbean and Latin America, built on around 3.0 million square meters within the resort Cap Cana, was officially opened in 2015 as part of several equestrian activities.

Stables Group president and developer Abraham Hazoury, accompanied by executive vice president Maria Amelia Hazoury, welcomed the quests.

"The world of horses has the virtue of being multidisciplinary: Jumping, Polo, Paso Fino, Race, Dressage, Reining, Enduro, Cross Country, among other disciplines which are contained within this deep passion and all of these will have a place in The Stables," said Maria Amelia Hazoury in her keynote speech, "We want to be a community that revolves around the horse, where members can share their admiration and common passion for this noble animal," she said, noting that The Stables is located within a broader community such as Cap Cana, "which will give you the opportunity to enjoy golf, fishing, the sea and many other complementary activities."

All these business developments on this amazing island are helping to boost the economy and attracting a high end type of tourist and these are the people that have the ability to see business opportunities there and are investing.

Latin America

Powered by a growing middle-class, the sales of luxury goods in Latin America have been experiencing considerable increase. In April 2014, Euromonitor reported that Latin America saw both a growth in sales and in the number of luxury goods outlets opening across the region. The report stated that over the last few years, this number has risen by almost 25%, which is significantly greater than any other region in the world.

Brazil tops the table of Latin America nations in terms of luxury sales. This sector, in Brazil alone, witnessed a 12% growth in 2013, a figure which translated into six times greater than the whole economy of the country. However, recently Brazil has been overtaken by some of its smaller neighbours in terms of domestic consumer appetite. Although Brazil's luxury retail infrastructure is booming with the likes of Burberry, Dolce and Gabbana and Yves Saint Laurent setting up their first shops in Latin America in São Paulo.

Mexico overtook Brazil as Latin America's largest luxury goods market back in 2012 and today it is the second biggest economy in Latin America and the fifth emerging economy after the BRIC nations. With a GDP of about $1.2 trillion Mexico is estimated to double its current number of high-income earners to 952,000 by the year 2030. Mexico's population is young and there is a booming middle class that in 2013 spent over $4 billion on apparel, accessories and wine proving that the wealth has begun to spread to secondary and tertiary cities.

Brands are beginning to take notice of Mexico and expanding their catchment areas by straying beyond the confines of department stores and are instead opening boutique shops offering home delivery services.

Mexico is now the world's second-biggest market for business jets, moving at a faster pace than Latin American rival Brazil, as it benefits from stronger economic growth.

While Mexico has long had a larger standing fleet, it had lagged behind Brazil in annual sales growth. That changed recently, according to Brazilian aircraft manufacturer, Embraer SA. The direction is likely to continue as Mexico's economy is projected to grow while Brazil is forecast to shrink.

Mexico, with only about half the population of Brazil, had 873 registered business jets at the end of 2014, topping the 854 for the South American country, according to JetNet's annual iQ report, which compiles aircraft data. Mexico's fleet grew by 4.8% last year, compared with Brazil's 3.6% increase.

Embraer believe so much in the Mexican market that they decided to open a sales office in the country. They already have one operations maintenance centre in Monterrey and are looking at installing a second one in or around Mexico City.

Mexico's standing as No. 2 in fleet size is due in part to its proximity to the U.S., which has the world's largest private aviation infrastructure and also the economic growth of Latin America.

For Embraer, Mexico represents a growth opportunity. It expects to expand its 2% market share there to 16% in the coming years, which is equivalent to Embraer's global executive jet market share.

The increase in business jet sales in Mexico can partly be attributed to fleet renewals, according to Embraer. Mexican jets tend to be older than Brazilian ones, with about 80% more than 10 years old, compared with 45% in Brazil. That presents a big replacement opportunity. Unfortunately, aging jets are seen as a safety risk especially after the 2012 crash of a 43-year-old Learjet that killed Mexican singer Jenni Rivera. An older jet can be safer than a new one if maintained and flown safely.

However, the Mexican market is ready for new jets. Previously, preowned business jets would go into Mexico after they had served in the U.S. That now has transitioned. It's almost completely new purchase activity.

One of these examples is recent acquisition of a Gulfstream G650 by Grupo Bal, replacing their 1988 Falcon 50.

However, the rising star of the Latin American economy is Colombia. In recent years the country has rebranded itself and is currently riding the wave to what could be one of the largest economies in Latin America. With new government policies reducing taxation and regulation, competitive industries and favourable demographics of Colombia, companies offering lower price points such as Sephora and Estee Lauder have been investing heavily in the country and are reaping the benefits. Luxury goods sales and the rise of the internet in the area has made items and their favourite brands, that were once only available abroad, appear in their department stores and at their doorsteps.

According to Wealth Insight, a research company, that claims that in recent times Colombia has created millionaires quicker than Brazil and Mexico. According to their report recently published and titled Colombia: Paisas and their Pesos: Colombia's prospering economy has created more millionaires over past five years than the world average. Volumes rose by 39%, whereas worldwide they declined by 0.3%... The 14,000 new millionaires created over the past five years put Colombia's total millionaire population at 35,900 at the end of 2012... There are 435 multimillionaires in Colombia, an increase of 49% from 292 individuals in 2007. The rise of wealthy individuals is a story common to many emerging economies.

But in a Colombia long-plagued by civil conflict, it has begun later than in some and from a lower base. "The rate at which millionaires are created is an influential indicator of the wider economy," says Wealth Insight's Oliver Williams. Certainly, the Andean country has made huge strides in the past decade in security as well as economic terms, turning into a hotspot for foreign investors. Some of Colombia's leading companies have endured rough times and in recent years have expanded abroad with market capitalisations enviable to many in the developed world. All of that appears to have contributed to the broadening of the top of the pyramid in Colombia—be it in number of millionaires (individuals with $1m or more) or multi-millionaires (individuals with $30m or more.

Wealth Insight anticipates Colombia to carry on creating millionaires at a record rate. The total number of Colombian millionaires is forecast to grow by 36%. However, Wealth Insight expects Colombian multimillionaire growth projected to increase 28%. The number of multimillionaires, however, will grow faster. Wealth Insight expects the number to increase by 36%.

And for the wealthier there has been a proliferation of high-end stores in cities such as Bogotá—from Montblanc to Maserati dealerships—in recent years.

Beyond Brazil, the future of the luxury market in Latin America is destined to grow, indicating the market is open for more business...

E-Commerce in Latin America

In Latin America, as much as in the rest of the world, e-commerce has come to stay. In 2019, it is estimated that the region housed 267.4 million digital buyers, a figure forecast to grow over 31% by 2024. Although the adoption of e-commerce in Latin America is still lower than in other emerging regions, online retail sales in this part of the world generated more than 70 billion U.S. dollars in 2019 and are expected to hit 116 billion by 2023. On a regional level, Brazil and Mexico compete for the spotlight, accounting for 32.5% and 28.8% of the Latin American e-commerce market, respectively. However, other economies such as Peru, Argentina and Colombia have been drawing increasing attention due to their steady growth.

In 2020, the COVID-19 outbreak marked a turning point in Latin America's online consumer behaviour. Confined to their homes, many people resorted to online shopping to supply their needs, activity which had, until then, been ruled out by a significant amount of the population. E-sales in Latin America grew by 230% during the first weeks after the declaration of the pandemic. The massive demand for home delivery boosted the growth of e-commerce segments that had already been gaining popularity in recent years, such as food and beverage. According to forecasts, food and personal care is expected to be the fastest growing e-commerce sector between 2019 and 2020. Finally, these changes seem to have transcended the coronavirus onset, becoming a normal habit in people's everyday lives. According to a survey conducted between March and April 2020, as much as 78% of the Latin Americans surveyed said they will continue to shop online after the pandemic.

Latin America is also part of the mobile shopping movement. In March 2016, 27% of internet users in Latin America used their mobile device to purchase a product or service via mobile device and 23% of internet users used an app to make a purchase. During an August 2016 survey, 43% of mobile buyers in Latin America stated that they purchased products via mobile on a monthly basis.

Quantum Economy Snippets

- Developing countries will grow nearly 7× faster than developed countries.
- More than 20 of the world's top 50 cities ranked by GDP will be located in Asia by the year 2050.
- Number of mobile-only internet users today=14 million, expected to grow 34% p.a. by 2030, connecting 60% of the world's population.

- Emerging-market middle class will double its share of global consumption (from a third to two-thirds) by 2050.
- Just over 60% of these new millionaires are coming from the Asia-Pacific region.
- Singapore has become financial capital of the Far East with businesses in robotics to watch.
- Japan's population reducing but opportunities in the tech space being created.
- Vietnam today is made up of 93.5 million people with average age of 30.3 years old. Vietnam is home to a new booming tech industry with a growing young population. The government has invested a lot of money in building new airports.
- North Korea offers $6 trillion dollars of mining resources and lots of new opportunities for business.
- By 2050 the UN predicts there will be 2.5 billion Africans, about a quarter of the global population.
- From 2000 to 2013, the number of millionaires on in Africa grew by more than 145% compared to the worldwide growth rate of 73%.
- African fashion designers are conquering the world and becoming the icons of the future.
- In 2034, Africa is expected to have the world's largest working-age population of 1.1 billion.
- More people in Africa are moving into cities. It is projected that Africa's consumers will spend USD $2 trillion by 2025.
- Smart phones are expected to be in the hands of 50% of the population by 2020 from only 2% in 2010.

- There are currently 350 large business jets operating in Africa and that figure is projected to grow to 960 by 2020.
- Tivat, Montenegro is becoming the new super-yacht hub of Europe and a place where more and more millionaires and billionaires are gathering and doing business.
- The Dominican Republic has the fastest growing economy in the Caribbean and certainly one to look into for investment and visiting with your private jet.
- Brazil, Mexico and Colombia are the three main economies in Latin America that are showing growth and offer interesting opportunities for the future.

Part Two: Why the Biz Jet is the Ultimate Twenty-first Century Business Tool

Chapter 4
Who and Why Are People Using Private Jets?

"If you are not actively seeking and creating opportunities which always contain an element of risk, you are actually exposing yourself to more serious risks in the long term."
—Tony Buzan

It's not so much the large corporations that are buying most of the private jets and using them but small companies. Most companies (59%) operating business aircraft have fewer than 500 employees and seven in 10 have less than 1,000 employees. Business aircraft users have a main presence on "best of the best" lists for the most innovative, most admired, best brands and best places to work, as well as dominating the lists of strongest companies in corporate governance and responsibility, revenue growth and market share, proving the point that business aviation is the sign of a well-managed global company.

In the post COVID-19 world we live in, the aviation and travel industry were the ones hit the most. Many airlines went bust and others resuming flights, with many cancelled routes and less frequency on others. This, coupled with people being afraid of catching a virus, is making High Net-Worth Individuals and corporations looking into private jet travel, leasing and ownership. With only 3.5% of UHNWIs owning their own jet, that number will certainly climb.

Saving Employee Time

Efficient employee scheduling and employee time-savings are possible because a private jet; has the ability to fly on demand and nonstop between smaller airfields that usually are closer to a traveller's destination than a major airport.

Increases Traveller Productivity, Safety and Security En-Route

When traveling on a biz jet, passengers can meet, plan and work in a secure office environment, free from interruptions and distractions, allowing them to discuss proprietary information without fear of a competitor anonymously sitting in the next row and eavesdropping on the conversation, industrial espionage or physical threat. Travellers can privately strategise before meetings and debrief afterwards or conduct meetings en-route. Also, many aircraft are outfitted with high-speed Internet access—that enable travellers to remain in constant contact throughout their flight with colleagues on the ground. Most importantly, the technology in the business jets is very advanced and often more modern than most airliners.

Flying into Airports Where Scheduled Airlines Don't

A study by Harris Interactive found that two-thirds of business jet flights are made into airports with infrequent or no scheduled airline service. In other words, without business aviation, the old saying, "You can't get there from here," would be a harsh reality for many companies.

Consider an ultra-affluent entrepreneur based in Guangzhou, China who wants to undertake a business and leisure trip to Europe with his core team.

He hopes to check on his wine vineyard investment in France, to visit his son who is studying at Oxford University in England, meet with some distributors and partners in London, play a round or two of golf at the Trump International Golf Links in Scotland, before heading to Russia to close a new oil deal. Quite a trip!

To our Chinese entrepreneur time is key, he has ambitious growth plans for his core business in Guangzhou and doesn't want to waste days negotiating his way through the trip on commercial airlines. It takes him just over 12 hours to fly direct from Guangzhou to Bergerac in France, to see how his winery investment is doing. He and his team are productive on the flight and arrive ready to do business. A quick jet from Bergerac over to Oxford and on the same day he is able to visit his son at University. Had he been relying on commercial flights he would have spent a frustrating nine-plus hours trying to connect between Bergerac and Oxford and would likely be somewhere over Europe, rather than enjoying a meal with his family.

A couple of days of meetings in London and it's time to experience the new Aberdeen based golf course developed by

Donald Trump. Direct flights save our business owner more than two and a half hours—key golfing time. Relaxed and refreshed from a few days spent in the fresh Scottish air, the last meeting of the trip is an oil deal in Tyumen, Russia. The flexibility of being able to fly direct once more saves a huge amount of time over 'airport hopping' with commercial airlines. The journey takes an afternoon, rather than a full day and with the contract signed it is time to return home.

In total the time spent in the air with direct flights is just under 28 hours; in contrast the time spent in the air, waiting in terminals and connecting via road with a commercial airline solution is over 83 hours. This will clearly impact the total time required to complete the trip. With a business jet the whole trip including family time, business meetings, wine tasting and several rounds of golf could be completed in just 8–10 days. The same trip completed using commercial airlines and making no allowance for the delays that 26% of all airline flights usually face, would take around 15 days. And as we must remember, "time is money."

Quantum Economy Snippets

> - A private jet has access to 10X more airports. There may be an airport minutes away from your meeting venue…
> - More small companies us private jets than large ones.
> - Work on the private jet with your team in complete safe, secure and confidential environment.
> - A business trip from China to Europe takes 28 hours flying (8–10 days) to complete by private jet, with

commercial airlines the same trip takes 83 hours (15 days).
- ➢ 26% of Commercial flights are delayed.

Chapter 5
Is a Private Jet Safe?

"Don't let the fear of losing be greater than the excitement of winning."

—**Robert Kiyosaki**

IN 2021 THERE WERE:
Airline Flights: 22.2M and 44 accidents.
Private Jet Flights: 1.6M. and 28 accidents.
Sources: IATA, Wing X, Flight Safety Foundation

CHANCES OF CRASHING:
Airlines: 0.00019%
Private Jets: 0.00175%

THEREFORE:

Flying with the airlines is 9.2X safer, than flying by private jet.

Let's look at the difference between an airline flight and one of a private jet.

COST OF FLIGHT LONDON, UK TO NEW YORK, USA

Airlines First Class: USD $10K
Private Jet Charter: USD $150K

The private jet flight is 15X that of flying First Class with the airlines but almost ten times more dangerous! Now, you could say that on that charter private jet there can be 6 passengers, reducing the cost to $25K × passenger and that is certainly a valid point.

However, if you are paying more shouldn't you be getting more and safety be top of the list?

According to Air Accident Investigators 88% of crashes were caused by human error. Accident records show repeated examples of crews skipping safety checks, working long days and overlooking hazards such as ice on the wings.

The NTSB investigators reported the pilots working for billionaire Lewis Katz, who was killed in 2014 when his Gulfstream GIV skidded off a runway, rarely did standard pre-flight safety checks. In a recent report issued by the NBAA, it was found that before take-off control check non-compliance among business aircraft operators is 17.66%. The U.S. NTSB found that the accident GIV crew did not perform a flight-control check before take-off, leaving them unaware that the gust lock was engaged. The aircraft crashed on take-off and all seven aboard died in the accident.

The NTSB recommended that NBAA work with industry on a study of the extent of non-compliance with pre-take-off flight control checks. The NBAA report—Business Aviation Compliance with Manufacturer-Required Flight Control Checks Before Take-off—analysed 143,756 business aviation flights between 1 January 2013 and 31 December 2015. It found that about 15% of those flights took off with only a partial flight control check and 2% without a full, valid check (defined as the stop-to-stop deflection of all flight controls per the aircraft flight manuals).

It is worrying that a highly experienced crew could attempt a take-off with the gust lock engaged, the data also revealed similar challenges across a variety of aircraft and operators. NBAA President and CEO Ed Bolen said, *"This report should further raise awareness within the business aviation community that complacency and lack of procedural discipline have no place in our profession."*

The NBAA report recommends operators establish flight-data monitoring programs. NBAA noted that only 1% of operators currently have such a program in place. The association also is urging operators to participate in safety-data collection programs such as Aviation Safety Information Analysis and Sharing System (ASIAS).

In 2001 a chartered jet crashed in Aspen, Colo., killing 18. According to NTSB reports, the passenger who paid for the flight was fuming after learning he might miss an airport curfew. This put pressure on the pilot, leading him to try landing, despite not being able to see the runway, investigators concluded. Unfortunately, biz jet pilots are subject to the whims of the people who pay them in a way pilots for airlines aren't.

The Aspen crash was one of 62 fatal accidents since 2000 involving the most-sophisticated models of corporate style jets and turboprops operated by professional pilots.

That compares with 13 for passenger airlines. Since 2007, there have been 106 fatalities on the smaller planes, compared with 50 on airlines, records show.

Airline crashes have become rare because carriers take steps to protect against pilot mistakes. Most Civil Aviation Authorities around the world don't regularly inspect many corporate aircraft operators and pilots are often left to decide when it's safe to land or how many hours they work.

When the Boss and/or Passenger Takes Over...

On private jets, one trend that often leads to catastrophe is when a passenger and/or boss overrides the pilot in making certain decisions. Not completing pre-flight checklists is probably one of the effects of passenger/boss pressure, often called "get there quick-itis."

I experienced passenger-pressure early in my career when I was flying with a newly qualified Captain and the passenger insisted, we land at St Moritz's airport, Samedan, in the Swiss Alps. That day there were storms in the vicinity and most of the valley was overcast. We took a chance and got in ok. However, we rushed to get the lead passenger's kids on-board together with their suitcases, as the storm was approaching the runway. The aircraft struggled to get airborne, once in the cruise I checked our weight and balance, to find we were loaded incorrectly. We had been in a rush to avoid weather and satisfy the passengers, compromising flight safety. In addition, once airborne we flew straight into the storm and the small Cessna Citation was rocked all over the place. After ten minutes of fighting our way above cloud everything calmed down. The lead passenger came to the flight deck to apologise for pushing us too far. I told him he could buy many things but he couldn't buy the weather...he agreed.

Core Facts

Among those who have died in small plane and helicopter crashes over the years: John F. Kennedy Jr, Stevie Ray Vaughan, John Denver, Ritchie Valens, singer Buddy Holly, Jiles "the Big Bopper" Richardson, Democratic Sen. Paul Wellstone of Minnesota, Russian Ice hockey player Lokomotiv Yaroslavl, golfer Payne Stewart, Mexican-American singer Jenni Rivera and Lewis Katz, a former owner of the NBA's New Jersey Nets and the NHL's New Jersey Devils, who died in summer 2014 and NBA superstar Kobe Bryant.

The National Business Aviation Association and the International Business Aviation Council (IBAC) say it's unfair to accuse the entire sector based on the behaviour of a small number of pilots. "For operators whose flight crews routinely adhere to industry best practices, the likelihood of a fatal accident is greatly diminished," says Peter Ingleton, a director at the Montreal-based IBAC.

Monkeys Flying Biz Jets...

So now you're probably thinking that private jet travel is dangerous. It is very safe and to some degree safer than the airlines. A lot will depend on the operator that you use. Before chartering a biz jet you need to ask the following questions:

What experience do the pilots have?

Where and what type of training have the crew had?

How and where is the maintenance done on the aircraft?

When you book a ticket with Virgin, British Airways or Lufthansa the answers to the above questions tell you that the standards are very high and therefore their flights safe. Private

Jet travel is on the increase and more and more operators are coming onto the scene. Using a broker to book your jet is a good idea but again they must have done their due diligence on the operators they use.

Personally, I am not a great fan of these new Apps selling seats on private jets or cheaper biz jet flights. Most of them are price driven, using operators that pay their pilots low salaries and/or cut corners on pilot training and maintenance, allowing them to sell aircraft cheaply, very often compromising flight safety.

In 2008 a chartered jet carrying employees of Kelso, a New York private equity firm, was speeding down the runway of an airport in New Jersey at almost 127 miles per hour when the plane failed to lift off.

The pilots hit the brakes and thrust reversers, sending the two-engine jet skidding across U.S. Route 46. The jet, a twin-engine Bombardier Challenger CL-600 trying to take off from New York Teterboro Airport in February 2005, wound up almost halfway inside a clothing warehouse, injuring all 11 people aboard and 3 on the ground. Once investigating the incident; it was found that the New York based broker had arranged the flight and vouched for the safety of the operator. A safety board analysis found that the aircraft operator was not authorised by the aviation agency to fly passengers. The safety board attributed the accident to the pilots' failure to ensure that the plane had been loaded within weight and balance limits and that the centre of gravity was properly adjusted. The human factor caused the accident and this was caused by a company cutting corners, paying pilots low salaries and obviously not attracting the right professionals.

You pay peanuts, you get the monkeys…

Quantum Economy Snippets

- There are 9.2X more fatal crashes on high-end corporate aircraft, than on passenger airlines.
- 88% of those crashes were caused by human error.
- 18% of private jet flights take-off without pilots completing pre-take-off checklist.
- Only 1% private jet operators have a Flight data Monitoring System in place.
- On the aircraft the Captain needs to be in charge, neither the boss nor the lead passenger.
- Make sure your pilots have solid background and pay them well. If you pay peanuts, you get the monkeys…

Chapter 6
Pilot Training and Selection

"The only thing worse than training your employees and having them leave is not training them and having them stay."
—**Henry Ford**

Both airline and private jet pilots go through the same flight schools. The recurrent flight simulator training and the standardisation may differ and this is where you need to make sure the biz jet guys have high standards.

However, a flight school qualifies you to fly for hire, it doesn't make you a pro. As a professional pilot I have flown in both worlds and have seen good and bad outfits in one and the other.

So, make sure you do your homework before you go on your next flight on a private jet.

The private jet offers you flexibility that the airlines will never be able to give you. Also consider if you buy your own jet, you will hire your own pilots. You will get to know them, this becoming a big plus. When you step onto an airliner more than often you don't even see the guys at the front. I remember once flying with a very careless Captain who kept missing items on the checklist, etc. Another pilot I flew with complained all day about his leave being cancelled and this distracted him affecting his performance on that day; also add in pilot fatigue, which is becoming one of the major factors, causing aircraft accidents. Airlines are struggling to make money and many regulators are permitting pilots to fly flat out, followed by minimum rest. These are factors that influence performance. If you know your pilots and look after them, chances are they will keep you a lot safer.

Loss **o**f **C**ontrol **I**n-**F**light (LOC-I) is another leading cause of aircraft crashes and crash-related fatalities worldwide. Rivalled only by **C**ontrolled **F**light **I**nto **T**errain (CFIT), LOC-I presents a unique challenge to professional aviation; it highlights a major deficiency in a pilot's ability to deal with several unusual fight attitudes and flight envelope excursions. Regrettably, current pilot training regulatory standards and certification requirements do not address this skill deficiency. However, the FAA in November 2013 finalised a new pilot training rule that will require airlines to provide pilots with "extended envelope" training in simulators by November 2018.

In a report issued by Boeing in July 2012, LOC-I represents the most severe cause factor in commercial aviation over the past 10 years, resulting in the most crash-related fatalities from 2002 through 2011—even more than CFIT.

Within a 10-year span, from 2004 through 2013, LOC-I was responsible for nearly 40% of all commercial aviation accidents. Business aviation statistics for LOC-I are slightly more prominent at roughly 45% of all fatalities being LOC-I.

The statistics provide extensive evidence that LOC-I is a significant risk in all flight operations across the entire spectrum of aviation sectors. As such, a flight department's Safety Management System (SMS) requires some form of mitigation for this identified risk. According to industry, one of the best ways to reduce the LOC-I threat is through a proven Upset Recovery Training Program (UPRT).

In May 2011 a pitch trim runaway incident involving a Falcon 7X in Malaysia, which caused Dassault to temporarily ground the 7X fleet. The report reveals how the crew recovered from an unusual and dangerous attitude.

The pilot flying used his military experience and applied a procedure he had learned for bombing. When the pitch angle increased rapidly, he rolled the aircraft sharply to the right, applying a 40- to 80-degree bank angle for about 20 seconds, according to the report. This decreased the pitch angle and stabilised the aircraft's speed.

The failure lasted two minutes and 36 seconds, after which the temperature of an electric motor exceeded its limit, triggering a bypass of the primary trim control system in favour of another chain of control. During this period, the tri-jet climbed from 13,000 to 22,000 feet and its calibrated airspeed dropped from 300 to 125 knots. The maximum pitch angle recorded was 41 degrees and the highest load factor was 4.6g.

This pilot's quick thinking converted the pitch angle into a turning manoeuvre, thus arresting the climb and stabilising speed. "The pilot had a very good reaction," Dassault chief test pilot Philippe Deleume reported. The manoeuvre was incorporated into Dassault's upset recovery training program in late 2014.

Sadly, an unsettling large number of business jet pilots today have never been in a fully developed stall or upset condition in the category and type of aircraft they're flying. I believe aerodynamic upsets are something every pilot carrying passengers should understand, experience and learn to successfully recover from. In the case of the Falcon 7X incident fortunately a former military pilot was on the flight deck and tapped into his training to save the day.

I don't believe the average private owner would be comfortable knowing their pilot lacked such training. Several high-profile accidents in business aviation and commercial airlines over recent years have brought significant attention to the need for additional training to fill a critical gap between simulator-based scenario training and hands-on inflight training using actual jet aircraft.

Providing your pilots actual training in prevention and recovery from upsets, rather than just exposure to extreme attitudes. While exposure helps make the all-attitude environment more familiar in some ways, only true UPRT 'training' programs provide the skills and proficiency needed to recover from real life situations, when a pilot needs those skills to be second nature to successfully fight and overcome the stress, fear and panic experienced in a real-world airplane upset situation.

A person who can perform a task in a predictable situation won't necessarily be able to perform that same task when surprised, according to new research published in *The International Journal of Aerospace Psychology*.

The study suggests that flight training should include elements of surprise.

The researchers used a motion-base flight simulator to test 20 airline pilots on their ability to recover from a stall in two situations.

"The goal of the study was to show that being skilful when you *are not* surprised and being skilful when you *are* surprised are two very different things," Landman told PsyPost.

"A surprise requires different mental processes and actions: it requires you to make sense of what is happening and react to the events. If you never practice this because you always train with predictable and scripted scenarios, then your trained skills may not hold up in an emergency. Those skills are said to be 'brittle' instead of resilient."

One pilot told the researchers, he had a different "mental image" of the upcoming task and had to quickly change his frame of mind after a surprise stall.

The study, like all research, has some limitations.

"The study merely showed that it's dangerous to ignore the challenges posed by surprising situations," Landman explained. "However, how to train pilots for these situations is still not very clear. Is it, for instance, necessary to surprise pilots during simulator training, or to train under stress? If so, to what extent?"

"Shortly, I will publish a study in which I compare simulator training that is very one-sided and predictable, with training that is more variable and unpredictable," she added. "The idea is that in unpredictable and variable training, you are forced to make sense of what is happening and you build better mental models. The results of this study are very promising. They suggest that including variability and unpredictability in simulator training is very helpful in teaching pilots how to deal with surprises."

Introducing extra pilot simulator training sessions, to cater for these unpredictable events, based on the type of operation is a way of keeping your pilots sharp and ready for any event.

So Why Have There Been a Significant Increase in Business Jet Accidents?

Pilot/owners do contribute to the poor safety record. This mainly happens because the owner is not a professional pilot and therefore lacks the depth of training. However, there are some owner pilots I have come across like entrepreneur, Jared Isaacman, who created a fleet of former military jets and got personally trained in these and in his various private jets. Over the years Jared built his flying experience up to a very high standard and recently became an astronaut, Commanding the First All-Civilian Space Mission on Space X, called Inspiration One (more about him in Chapter 13). On the other spectrum there are people that have cut corners, just to be able to fly their own jet and have lost their lives and others, due to their lack of humility…

The average airline pilot is flying into well serviced airports and flying the same 30–40 routes. With many airports to fly into, the private jet pilot is flying into far more destinations, often enough these airports are not well equipped. My incident flying into St Moritz Airport, early on in my career, is a classic example of the challenges these small airports present. Combine this with boss/passenger pressure and you get a recipe for disaster.

In the airline world it is always said that airplanes make money when in the air and cost money when on the ground. The same is said about the pilots. In private jet charter world, the same rule applies. However, if you own a biz jet, this asset will make you money 24/7; as long as you continuously use it as a business tool. The ability to decide to travel somewhere and actually get into the air in a few hours gives you power, which turns into money.

The problem lies in the fact that these private jets don't fly as often. An average airliner flying 4,000 hours a year, compared to the average private jet flying 250 hours...

Also, if you own your own jet a great way of using it as a business tool is sending the jet out to pick people up and fly them into see you. The London based brothers, Nick and Christian Candy do this with their Challenger 605 jet. They would send the jet out to the Middle East to bring in potential clients and show them their high-end Real Estate for sale. So don't just think in terms of where you can travel to but also how the jet can bring people into see you.

With the internet and modern Apps on people's mobile devices the private jet charter market has become a lot more competitive and unfortunately this is mostly price driven. Often in private aviation cheap is synonymous to dangerous, so before booking your charter make sure you do your due diligence on the company that operate the aircraft or use a broker that vets the operators properly.

The Parable of the Soccer Player

Imagine you just bought a soccer team and decided to buy top player, Cristiano Ronaldo. Ronaldo is considered the best player in the world. First, being a top player, he will want to be paid very well for his services. Next thing is you will have to give him the best training, to enable him to perform at his best on the field.

When talking to clients about buying a private jet I always emphasise that the right pilots are just as important. Hire right, provide them with more training than the regulatory minimum requirements, include Upset Recovery training and above all make sure you don't tire them out. After spending millions on a jet you want to make sure that who you hire to fly you around is going to be performing safely. Just like a top soccer player, to attract them you need to offer a good package and top training to help them improve and always do their best.

Should I Charter My Jet Out?

I generally discourage jet owners chartering their planes out to others. Some aircraft management companies will tell you this will pay for your own flights. If you're lucky you'll recuperate 10% of your costs but end up putting more hours on your airplane, increasing the depreciation.

To better illustrate this point, I want to tell you about a friend of mine who was flying the Dassault Falcon 7X, 650–700 hours a year literally all over the globe. He was always telling me how tired he is. If his boss were to not charter the aircraft to third party companies, my friend would have flown 400 hours a year and been well rested for his boss' flights. So, after spending USD $60M on a jet, do you really want to be putting your life at risk by being jetted around the skies by fatigued pilots?

Quantum Economy Snippets

- Hire Pilots with a solid background.
- Hire Pilots that will fit your type of operation.
- Provide your pilots with more Simulator training than regulators minimum requirements.
- Send your Pilots for Upset Recovery Training.
- Leave the Decisions on the Aircraft to the Pilots, don't push your crew into unsafe territory.
- Above average pay attracts above average pilots.
- Operate your aircraft privately, do not charter to third party.
- Make sure your Pilots are well rested, so they can ALWAYS give you their BEST performance and keep you safe.

Chapter 7
Why Private Jet Travel Will Increase

"You never change things by fighting the existing reality. To change something, build a new model that makes the existing model obsolete."

—**R. Buckminster Fuller**

1. The Internet is Driving More International Business

According to eMarketer the Philippines and India will lead the world in retail ecommerce sales growth this year, with respective increases of 25.9% and 25.5%. Countries in Latin America and Southeast Asia will make up most of the top 10 list, while the last spot will go to the US, the only advanced economy to slide into the rankings, with 15.9% growth.

Beyond the chart: None of the Western European countries we track will see a double-digit growth rate starting this year and through the end of our forecast period in 2025. By contrast, ecommerce sales will climb at those rates in every market we break out in Latin America.

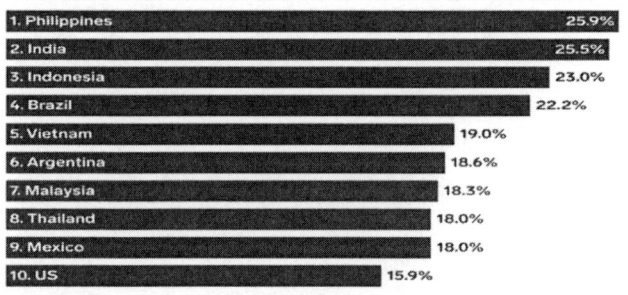

2. It is Easier to Start Businesses Today

When I left my career as an airline pilot to become an aviation entrepreneur in 2012, I was working mainly from home and travelling to see clients and inspect aircraft if and when needed. With very little money I got a website up and running and then started calling people I knew and networked online. Many people thought I had venture capital behind me but in reality, I didn't. Pulling this off even 10 years ago would have been impossible, without serious financial backing. Having no money to start, I leveraged on technology using tools like zoom video, my YouTube channel Biz Jet TV and LinkedIn.

3. The Wealthy are on the Increase

Underpinning luxury's extraordinary growth has been the advance of wealth globally. All the various Wealth Reports out there all point in the direction of the UHNWIs increasing my approximately 5,000 per year.

People are also becoming wealthy at a younger age. Call it the Mark Zuckerberg trend. In the 1960s, almost half of the wealthiest Americans were senior citizens. Now less than 40% of the super-rich are over 65, according to a recent report by economists Emmanuel Saez and Gabriel Zucman. What is less clear is whether the young and wealthy are self-made, new money or beneficiaries of old money. "There may be more Mark Zuckerbergs at the top of the wealth distribution than in the 1960s but also more Paris Hiltons," Saez and Zucman write.

Due to its rapid economic gains, China's wealth boom has occurred over the last decade. As a result, most of the country's richest citizens are young and experiencing wealth for the first time. This is in direct contrast to countries such as the UK and US, where more money has accumulated by being passed down from generation to generation.

This new Chinese elite are also younger than their counterparts in Europe and North America. The average age of the high net-worth group is between 40-years old and 50-years old, compared with 50- years old and 60-years old in other countries.

4. Airport Security

We all read about the Russian Airbus A321 that exploded over Egypt in October 2015. The investigations pointed towards a bomb as the cause. The political instability and terrorism in the Middle East are fuelling an increase in terrorism worldwide. Airline travel is becoming more tedious with stricter security checks in airport, where passengers are having to pitch-up at the airport sometimes three hours before a flight.

James Woolsey, former director of the CIA, made a shocking statement recently on Fox News that many of the nation's airport security staffers are not subjected to full vetting. Many come from overseas locations and are hired through the same process used to employ farm workers, he said. In other words: they're not subjected to background checks that could alert to terror ties. "They used to be vetted," Woolsey said in an interview on "America's Newsroom," "Now, quite a few of them are foreign nationals who have just worker visas. They're treated like agricultural workers." Woolsey acknowledged he didn't know if the "Transportation Security Administration (TSA) actually hired foreign workers. But he said a private company that provides security at more than a dozen of the nation's ports has hired lots of foreign workers that are not vetted."

5. More Terrorism

Almost 18,000 people were killed in terrorist attacks in 2013, a 61% increase from the 2012. Four terrorist groups, the Islamic State, Al-Qaeda, the Taliban and Boko Haram were responsible for two thirds of all such deaths around the globe.

The Global Terrorism Index, produced by the London based Institute for Economics and Peace, also found that 80% of terrorist attack fatalities occurred in only five countries: Afghanistan, Iraq, Nigeria, Pakistan and Syria. Worryingly, the 63% increase from 11,133 terrorist deaths in 2012 to

17,958 in 2013 is the biggest year-on-year escalation since records began in 2000.

Since the turn of the millennium, the number of deaths due to terrorist activates has increased fivefold, which also coincided with US military campaigns in Afghanistan and Iraq. With aircraft and airports being a target, like we recently saw in Turkey and Brussels, this is encouraging more HNWIs to either charter private jets or even better own their own aircraft. Owning your own jet from a security standpoint is far better as you control everything from pilot hiring, training, maintenance, etc.

6. Providing More Flexibility and Speed

We all know that entrepreneurs and business owners have to think fast to survive. Speed is in their DNA, moving quickly instinctively to them. Still, it's difficult to overstate the importance of this in business. With business aviation allowing more efficient, flexible, safe, secure and cost-effective access to destinations across the world. Airlines access 400 airports in the USA, while private jets can get into another 5,000+ smaller airports, similar statistic in Europe with the business aircraft opening you up to +4,200 airports, compared to the 350 serviced by the airlines. With employees being able to hold confidential meetings in the air, plan and work with each other aboard business aircraft, research proves productivity en-route is enhanced 20% compared to when in the office. In many situations business aviation is the best or only transportation option available, opening the door to global commerce for small-community and rural populations by linking them directly to population centres and manufacturing facilities. Studies have also shown that business aviation contributes greatly to local economies across the world.

Business aircraft allow employees to make a trip involving stops at several locations, then return to headquarters the same day. Hundreds or thousands of dollars can be saved on hotel rooms, rental cars, meals and other expenses that would be needed to make the same trip over several days via auto, train or airline transport.

A study, conducted by NEXA Advisors, shows that by taking into consideration a number of variables, companies using business aviation outperform those without aircraft by 70%. According to the study, business aircraft users had a dominant presence, on average of 92%, among the most innovative, most admired, best brands and best places to work, as well as dominating the list of companies' strongest in corporate governance and responsibility. The report also finds that business aviation alone is the only asset capable of accelerating strategic transactions, consequently, providing a competitive edge to top performing companies.

The study also examined whether the use of business aircraft provided benefits to small and medium businesses, measured in terms of shareholder and enterprise value. NEXA Advisors applied the same methodologies in its first volume "Business Aviation: An Enterprise Value Perspective," published in 2017. With this study, NEXA has extended its sample size to examine small and medium enterprises that used business aviation to better compete and grow their businesses. The analysis showed that small and medium companies in America that used business aviation consistently outperformed nonusers.

In 2014 the NBAA conducted a study on private jet usage. Contrary to popular belief, only 22% of passengers on business aircraft are top management, compared to about 50% who are mid-level managers and 20% who are technical, sales, or service staff. Interestingly, only 3% of US business aircraft are flown by Fortune 500 companies. The rest are flown by the government, universities and smaller businesses. The study showed that 59% of companies operating business aircraft have less than 500 employees and about 70% have less than 1,000 employees. Most of these aircraft are small—the majority seat six passengers and fly less than 1,000 miles. So, overall good times ahead for the private jet industry.

Quantum Economy Snippets

- Internet is driving more international business.
- Easier and cheaper to start businesses today.
- Wealthy are on the Increase. There are more opportunities for wealth creating in the twenty-first century.
- Airport security being enhanced causing door to door time of air travel to increase.
- There was a 61% increase in terrorist attacks between 2012 and 2103. Sadly, terrorism is on the increase.
- People 20% more productive when working on a private jet than when in the office. Productivity decreases 40% when traveling by commercial airline.
- Flying private gives more flexibility and speed.

Chapter 8
Should I Buy New or Pre-Owned

"*An entrepreneur is someone who jumps off a cliff and builds a plane on the way down.*"

—**Reid Hoffman**

Most people think they must buy a new jet and spend USD $50M because they perceive an older jet as dangerous. Having been a pilot for over 30 years a good and safe airplane has nothing to do with age but ALL to do with reliable and professional maintenance and efficient piloting techniques.

New can really make sense if according to your tax jurisdiction you can write-off the depreciation and you are planning to fly over 500–600 hours a year. However, I do recognise that some people just can and therefore want the latest new aircraft built, just like people queue-up for the latest iPhone because they can. However, if you are not in the "*just because I can*" category you must go about your choice in a systematic way.

Buying an older aircraft and giving it a good makeover is the way some people are going these days. For example, instead of spending +USD $35M on a newer Gulfstream G550 why not buy a pre-owned Bombardier Global Express and refurbish it all for under USD $8M. Most people look at buying a jet when they plan on flying 200–250 hours a year. I say buy a jet; even if you will be only flying 100 hours a year, because it will give you the exponential edge. Turn the jet into your Ultimate twenty-first century Business tool. As well as the flexibility you will gain from this you will also be well away from any terrorist, as you will know all the people flying with you.

Another option is to lease a pre-owned jet for 3–36 months.

This gives you all the benefits of ownership without having to outlay large amounts of cash. Use the jet for a year to grow your business and put you in the position of buying your own jet once the lease is up. This is the type of service we developed with one of my companies, where we go out and buy and refurbish older biz jets and either resell them, put them out on a straight lease or on a Try Before You Buy, lease program.

In choosing an older jet you will need to seek professional advice. As there are many aircraft on the pre-owned market, sifting through aircraft spec sheets and knowing what has been selling and at what price is key into finding a good deal.

What Are the Chinese Up To?

If we look at the Chinese market, before 2013 nearly everyone buying a biz jet were buying new. The private jet was seen as a luxury item, so you needed to have a brand new spanking shiny jet on the tarmac to impress everyone.

Chinese buyers are learning quick and have become more mature and practical, realising the real advantages of a pre-owned airplane.

A pre-owned biz jet market has emerged in China in the past three years. In 2015 the number of business jets rose by 59 to 439 in the Greater China region, which includes the mainland, Hong Kong, Macau and Taiwan. Preowned aircraft represented 27% in the additions to the Greater China fleet during the previous year and I predict this number will increase exponentially over the next few years. For most buyers, pre-owned aircraft are attractive because of their availability and pricing. In today's aviation industry, it can take up to two years to deliver a custom-made business jet once an order has been received. Buyers who order, for example, a popular aircraft such as a Gulfstream G650, would be lucky to take delivery three years after deposits were made.

Not only is this time-consuming but also leads to higher costs of capital since the buyers need to prepay tens of millions of dollars to the manufacturer.

Getting a good deal is also an important reason for Chinese buyers to consider a pre-owned jet. As a very general rule of thumb, a biz jet depreciates about 5% a year. This will also depend on how many hours it flies and what the market is like. Although demand for private jets in China was suppressed by the anti-corruption campaign for a while, this market is far from saturated. With the number of Chinese billionaires increasing and the realisation that the biz jet is much more of a business tool than a luxury item more and more entrepreneurs from China will be getting their own jets.

Quantum Economy Snippets

- Age of a jet is not as important as the way it is maintained and the way it is flown.
- An older refurbished jet can be a good solution if you plan on flying 100–150 hours a year.
- Why not lease a pre-owned Biz jet for 12 months?
- A new jet only makes sense if you are planning on flying a high number of hours or you have certain tax breaks.
- Choice between old and new depends on your specific circumstance, getting professional advice on this is key.

Part Three: Business Cases for a Faster Future

Chapter 9
Wal-Mart, Tesco and Private Jets

"Getting rich is the result of doing things in a certain way"
—**Wallace D. Wattles**

In 1945, former J. C. Penney employee, Sam Walton, purchased a branch of the Ben Franklin stores from the Butler Brothers. His strategy was to sell products at low prices to get higher-volume sales at a lower profit margin, with the consumer in mind. Faced with the challenge of high lease price and branch purchase, he was still able to find lower-cost suppliers than those used by other stores. He passed on the savings in the product pricing, winning over more customers than his competitors. Wal-Mart founder, Sam Walton used a frugal approach as he built his Supermarket chain.

What many do not know is that use of private aircraft was key to Sam Walton's business strategy in building his empire. He was a private pilot and used his Cessna C414 to travel around Arkansas and neighbouring states to visit his stores, scout new locations and recruit staff. Being based in Bentonville, Arkansas and in the early days there was no interstate highway there. An early road trip to visit another store could take 8 hours but a short plane flight could cut that down to 1 hour. To build the business, Sam built a fleet of airplanes to be used as business tools. With more than 11,695 stores and clubs in total over 28 countries, Wal-Mart's travel program takes employees to locations all over the world-cities and towns not always closely served by commercial airports. While the world's largest retailer relies heavily on airlines, the company also operates 22 private jets, comprising part of the largest corporate fleet in the world, according to director of global travel services Duane Futch.

Walmart encourages their people to fly commercial airlines when a direct flight is available-given the high demand for corporate aircraft and higher operating margins-its corporate fleet has become a source of relief for time-strapped associates needing to get in and out of stores on short notice.

"Efficiency of time is one of the main reasons we have the corporate fleet," Futch said, *"but if someone is traveling to a city where we have nonstop airline service out of Northwest Arkansas Regional Airport, which is our home airport, we will ask that person to go on the airlines rather than use the company jet. We think that's more efficient use of money and more efficient use of the corporate fleet."*

While many companies reserve corporate jet usage for its most senior executives, Futch said regional vice presidents-typically responsible for up to 500 stores and division vice presidents-each responsible for roughly 100 stores-and their teams are the most frequent flyers on corporate aircraft. This makes use of planes less about status and more about need, Futch noted.

The Walmart executives very rarely have to stay overnight and travel on their jets to multiple locations in one day. However, when they do night-stop they have to share hotel rooms to keep costs down. For a lot of companies, the benefits of the corporate aircraft far outweigh the costs. "*Wal-Mart is probably the most penny-pinching, efficient company on the planet*," says Chris MacDonald an ethics expert and visiting professor at the Keck Graduate Institute in Claremont, California.

The Walmart fleet of Private Jets is made-up mostly of Learjets that carry up to 10 people with a range of around 2,200 miles, one Global Express and one Global 5000 with intercontinental range aircraft.

Jack Cohen, the son of Jewish migrants from Poland, founded Tesco in 1919 when he began to sell war-surplus groceries from a stall at Well Street Market, Hackney, in the East End of London. The Tesco brand first appeared in 1924. Tesco was floated on the London Stock Exchange in 1947 as Tesco Stores (Holdings) Limited. During the 1950s and the 1960s Tesco grew organically and also through acquisitions, until it owned more than 800 stores.

Tesco has expanded internationally and also into other businesses, creating Tesco Bank and Telecoms. Like Walmart, Tesco owned and operated a fleet of private jets. Through a UK-based subsidiary called Kansas Transportation, which was established in 2005 to obtain better terms from suppliers of aircraft and fuel.

Financial statements filed by Kansas Transportation show that its income rose from £2.3m in the year to February 2009 to £8.99m in the year to February 2012, the last available period.

Tesco was operating in 14 overseas markets since 2005 and has doubled its annual profits from £1.8bn to £3.8bn over that period. After its most disastrous year in 95 years in business, in September 2014 Tesco appointed former Unilever executive, Dave Lewis as CEO. The new CEO decided to sell all five of Tesco's private jets because they gave the wrong image. It is sad to see that in Europe the private jet is seen ONLY as a luxury item and not as a BUSINESS TOOL. It is quite evident that Walmart's use of private jets, as a business tool, has been key in making Walmart MUCH BIGGER and PROFITABLE than Tesco.

	Years in Business	Stores	Countries	Turn-over	EBIT
Tesco	98	6,351	13	$74bn	$3.8bn
Walmart	71	11,695	28	$483bn	$124.6bn
Difference	27 years	+5,344	+15	+$409bn	+$120.8bn

Source: Wikipedia based on 2017

In Europe, we have a lot to learn from our American cousins, as far as private jets and business is concerned. Business and entrepreneurship are not perceived as a positive thing in Europe, while in America kids are taught to think big and make dreams come true. Back in Europe kids are encouraged to get a job and live within their means.

Quantum Economy Snippets

➢ A private jet if used in a certain way can become a great wealth multiplier.

➢ A private jet can be used to move teams of people through multiple locations in one day.

Chapter 10
Does Flying by Biz Jet Increase Sports Performance?

"Time is the most valuable asset you don't own. You may or may not realise it yet but how you use or don't use your time is going to be the best indication of where your future is going to take you."

—**Mark Cuban**

Pro-athletes' performance is always being measured and even a minor change can dramatically change results. In the 2012 European Soccer Championships after a stellar tournament the Italian national team lost to Spain in the final, 4-0. Interestingly the Italians had travelled nearly 4,200 miles (6,700km) more than their opponents.

A study of travel in Major League Baseball competition found that teams had a 61% chance of winning when their opponent crossed 3 time zones.

The only professional league—so far—to feature regular long-haul travel is Super Rugby, which features teams from Australia, New Zealand, South Africa, Argentina and Japan. Founded in 1996, the league's development holds important lessons for us air travellers. In the five years when the league included 14 teams, the home side won 61% of the time, at the high end of most professional leagues. Travel appears to be a significant factor—home teams facing an opponent from the same country won 54% of their games, versus 64% against teams from abroad. South African professors found that hosting a team from abroad was worth 4.5 additional points, or around half of the average home-team scoring advantage over the period.

Back in the USA over the past 15 seasons in the National Football League, visiting teams that travel less than 1,000 miles won 43% of their games, versus 40% when travelling 2,000 miles or more. An older study found statistical significance only among west coast teams, who saw their away-game winning percentage fall by 16% when playing on the east coast, compared with travelling within their home time zone.

Formula One drivers and professional tennis and golfers probably travel internationally even more. For a pro-golfer the difference between winning and coming second or qualifying for their tour card versus missing out can come down to the smallest of margins.

From week to week, a huge number of variables place demands on them, their bodies and their performance. Thanks to modern technology these variables can be closely looked at and fully understood. For most people (and particularly athletes) the body responds well to and likes routines, structure and balance. As a professional golfer travelling the world with the modern international schedule of golf, this can sometimes be very hard to achieve.

Sleep patterns among professional golfers can be hugely variable due to time zone changes, jet lag, very early or very late tee times, media requirements and travel delays to name a few. We know that sleep is a crucial factor in human physical and mental health and performance. To a certain extent there are similarities between the lifestyle of pro-golfer, the pilot and an international businessman. Main difference being the pro-golfer gets plugged into with technology to monitor performance. For a professional golfer flying privately all season, can mean just over 100 hours in the air, costs around USD $0.5M.

The world's top 30 golfers, make at least $6 million a year between prize money and endorsements, for them flying private is a no-brainer. The players in the tier below tend to text around and find two, or, better, three other golfers to "jet-pool" together, this brings the cost to most destinations to about the same as a first-class ticket. Obviously, coordinating everyone's schedule can get complicated but the tour has travel staff to help.

If you miss the cut Friday morning and want to hop on a flight that afternoon to West Palm Beach, you won't have a problem. Tons of pros live there. If you need to go to Phoenix or Dallas, fly commercial. There are so many direct flights that you'll get there in the same amount of time.

Most professional golfers are on the road a lot so having your own jet means you can take your family with you at no extra cost. The psychological toll of moving a family with two or three kids through a crowded security line is no way to prepare for a tournament. You can drive up to the jet, load your bags right away and off you go!

Many golfers fly private, to cut down on distractions. Getting in the right frame of mind to compete against the best in the world is hard enough without having to deal with delays, lost bags, grubby food courts and other people's screaming kids.

Former female world #1 golfer, Annika Sorenstam said she became a lot more productive when she started flying by private jet. She felt rested and found it no hassle. She was more on time, too. Sorenstam worked on the plane and prepared in a peaceful environment. Most people think it's expensive but when you see the outcome, the increase in performance pays for the plane. Therefore, the top 30 professional golfers today all travel by private jet, most of them owning their own.

When Mark Cuban became the majority owner of the Dallas Mavericks in 2000, the team hadn't had a winning season in 10 years. And because the team was awful, very few people were going to games.

One of the first things Cuban did when he took over the club was buy them a VVIP Boeing B757. This way they now controlled their own schedule, the food on board, had a lower cabin altitude and all the other advantages of biz jet travel. It took Cuban until 2013 to make the Mavericks profitable but since he took over, the Mavs have made the playoffs all but one year since 2001 and have sold out every game since 15 December 2001.They won their first NBA championship in 2011 and the way they travel by air has played a key role.

When talking to potential private jet clients I always talk about the health benefits and how that effects business performance. The aircraft may seem expensive to buy and manage but you have to look at the increased business performance it brings, just like the professional athlete sees it bring him or her more wins.

Even top soccer player Cristiano Ronaldo has joined the ranks of private jet owners. He purchased a pre-owned Gulfstream G200 and uses it to visit friends and do business in between matches. His jet has improved his lifestyle big-time and this is allowing him to do more business deals and keep up top performance on the pitch.

One Oxford Economics report estimates that around 10% of the revenue generated from business-related trips can be attributed to business aviation. In addition, private jet users are more successful at delivering value to their shareholders. In fact, according to the NBAA Business Aviation Fact Book 2014, business jet travellers generated 245% higher return for their shareholders (dividends plus stock price appreciation) than those travelling by other of transportation.

Quantum Economy Snippets

- If you are travelling with airlines across 3 time zones to play a match you have 61% chance of losing.
- Formula One drivers and pro-golfers both compete extensively across the globe. To be at the top in their sport travelling by private jet is key.
- Most of the world's top 30 golfers are private jet owners. They all claim that as well as being a great time saver it also gets them to new tournaments well rested, a key to staying at the top of your game.
- Dallas Mavericks have always made the NBA playoffs since flying their own private jet. The extra

legroom, customised menus, flying on their schedule (not the airlines) and simple private comfortable environment, all add together to help improve overall performance. We all know that better performance in sports, turns into more dollars…

- Business jet travellers generate higher returns for their shareholders.

Chapter 11
Where the Private Jet Can Allow Business, Your Hobby and Charity; All Work Together

"Many highly intelligent people are poor thinkers. Many people of average intelligence are skilled thinkers. The power of a car is separate from the way the car is driven."
—Edward de Bono

Don Catalano joined the US Army out of High School and eventually found himself serving in the Special Forces HALO scuba team. This experience really shaped him, helping him realise how a small team can be more powerful and effective than a large team.

After his experience in the military, Don began a career in Real Estate and took up flying as a hobby. Today he is President and CEO of his own Real Estate brokerage called iOptimize Realty (www.ioptimizerealty.com), with his flying playing a part in his professional success.

Don's company is a Commercial Real Estate (CRE) specialist representing tenants, not landlords. By analysing property metrics, the company's dedicated tenant representatives regularly achieve rents 30% below market using iOptimize's proven and proprietary systems. They also work with a global network of commercial real estate advisors to find the best deals.

In 2007, the iOptimize Realty team foresaw the economic tsunami and subsequent rollback of market rents. Don and his team showed their clients how much over-market their CRE portfolios had become and offered an easy way to optimise them. Today, they are doing this again in light of the Covid-19 pandemic.

The company's unique take on the CRE market accommodates client needs in secondary and tertiary markets that most other firms don't want to work within.

It was twenty-five years ago that Don bought his first airplane, a Mooney piston single and started using it for business. Flying his Mooney to visit clients, he soon realised how the airplane was becoming a valuable business tool.

Eventually, his work required trips further afield and he upgraded to a Piper Meridian single-engine turboprop before purchasing the twin-engine Light Jet he flies today: A Honda jet Elite.

Dan's business focusing on commercial Real Estate during the Covid lockdowns necessitated a change in the way he did business. With his small team working from home, iOptimize Reality began showing clients property via video-conferencing technology.

Virtual visits only worked to a certain extent, however and Don upped his game by flying the HondaJet to pick up certain clients to fly them to see Real Estate in person.

Don mentions how mindsets have changed and working from home is going to be okay for some jobs, "A hybrid work model is going to be okay. But where there might have been reluctance from prospective customers and clients to take the corporate jet in the past (i.e., 'is it ok to take the corporate jet, or should we take the airlines?' that reluctance is gone)."

"Imagine the conversation between boss and employee," he illustrates: 'I really need you to go and look at that 50,000 sq. ft office in Boca Raton, because we are moving out of New York.'

"Sure, I'll do that, boss but my last flight was cancelled and I don't want to wear a mask for three hours—can I use this company that has its own private jet?"

Don is seeing an increase in the usage of his jet to the point where, if the trend continues, his company will eventually acquire a second plane. He explains that iOptimize has always had the company aircraft built into its business strategy, as a tool, for twenty years. Now the company is ramping up its usage, the business is growing exponentially.

"The demand and the utility have changed from the plane being a 'nice to have' item, to becoming a necessity," he shares.

Though Don doesn't charge his clients for using the jet, nor increase his fees in any way, he's clear that the deal does need to have enough substance in it to justify deploying the HondaJet. It costs Don's company just over $3,000 per hour to operate the aircraft, so a trip may cost iOptimize $20,000, which Don considers an investment into the deal that he's happy to cover.

Combining Business With Piloting

So how does Don combine being both the CEO and the pilot of the HondaJet? Clients are always impressed that Don is not only a smart businessman but also flies the company jet.

Realising that flying is a life and death activity, he says if you're going to do the flying—especially carrying clients and employees—you need to be trained at a professional level to be safe. He goes over and above in this regard, visiting Flight Safety twice a year for recurrent training and soon will be adding Upset and Recovery Prevention Training (URPT) as part of his annual training routine.

He had already flown 4,000hrs before attempting to obtain a Type Rating in the HondaJet, having spent eighteen years flying the Piper Meridian in IFR.

According to Don, Covid has caused a paradigm shift in the workplace and companies have realised that working from home can be very cost-effective. Consequently, the need for large corporate offices in the centre of London or New York are becoming less necessary.

Homeworking will only get you so far, though, before a face-to-face meeting becomes necessary. That's when owning your own jet becomes key.

"Private jet usage is now becoming very acceptable, as it should be, it is a tool, a magic carpet," Don says. *"It allows point-to-point travel, which is something that is becoming more difficult now with [the airlines], where you often need to fly via Point B to get from A to C."*

"The private jet takes you from A to C [direct, saving] time and hassle and is a lot more comfortable."

Charitable Flying

Don also flies his jet for charity. When thirteen-year-old Owen Sherman needed a lift to get to Shriners Children's Hospital in Springfield, Massachusetts, to receive his two new prosthetic legs, Don helped out, volunteering to fly his HondaJet Elite.

He took off from Republic Airport, flew to Bangor, Maine to pick up the Shermans and flew them to Springfield where Owen underwent surgery. Then he flew them back to Bangor before flying home to Long Island.

Don volunteers as part of the Patient Airlift Services (PALS) charity flight team, donating his time and cost of the flights. A veteran charity flyer, he's piloted more than two dozen charity flights in the last few years.

All-in-all, some great perspectives from Don, from how to use a private jet as a business tool and also how to go about it, if you choose to also be the pilot.

Quantum Economy Snippets

- ➢ Don Catalano learnt in the military that a small team can be more powerful and effective than a large team. He applied this lesson into his Real Estate business.
- ➢ Don uses his jet to pick clients up and this is increasing deal flow.
- ➢ Don flies himself and does lots of extra training, in order to fly to a high professional standard.
- ➢ Your private jet can also be a great tool to use in reaching out to others. Use your jet for charity.

Chapter 12
Building a Restaurant Empire by Private Jet

"As much as you need to know your operations, if you don't understand the finance side and how to do the business, you're never going to be successful. So you might be the best operator or visionary but if you don't understand the finance side... I'm successful because I know the finance side but I also know operations; it's not an accident."

—Tilman J. Fertitta

Tilman Fertitta purchased Landry's in the 1980s and has since grown it into an empire of more than 600 properties in the U.S. and abroad, spanning 14 different countries. In addition to Golden Nugget Casinos, Fertitta's empire comprises dozens of restaurant brands including Landry's, Rainforest Café,' McCormick and Schmick's, Del Frisco's Double Eagle Steakhouse, Bubba Gump Shrimp Co. and Saltgrass Steak House. He also owns the Houston Rockets NBA basketball team. Fertitta, whose net worth is estimated at $8 billion, was also the star of the CNBC reality series "Billion Dollar Buyer," and now makes regular appearances on the network's news program "Power Lunch." In 2019, his debut book, *Shut Up and Listen: Hard Business Truths That Will Help You Succeed*, landed on *The New York Times*' Best Sellers list.

His First Private Jet was a Key Milestone

For Fertitta, there was a specific moment when he felt like he had made it.

"I always had a goal to buy my first plane at 35 years old," Fertitta said. He started with a Cessna Citation 500 and then worked his way up to his two Gulfstream G550s, that he owns and operates today.

The purchase of the plane also served as an investment in his business.

"When I was growing my company in the beginning, having that plane made it so easy to look for locations across the country," Fertitta says.

Being able to travel easily is a must when growing a national brand, according to the billionaire.

"It's how I do everything I do, being able to leave when I want to leave, go home when I want to go home," Fertitta says. *"I could not cover near as much ground [without it]."*

Surviving to Thriving in the Covid Lockdowns

In March 2020, when Covid-19 lockdowns began, Fertitta shutdown nearly all his operations and laid off 40,000 workers (he says he has since refilled all but 3,000 positions.) His companies laid off 70% of their staff. His restaurants were bringing in just four to five percent of their usual business. He took steps to support workers and keep the restaurants afloat. In 2018 Fertitta had placed a bet by investing $308 million in food delivery company Waitr, he saw the lockdowns as an opportunity to grow this business, which in turn offered jobs to furloughed Landry's employees. He received $160 million in forgivable federal paycheck protection program loans but then gave it back to Uncle Sam after many had protested.

By April 2020, a more aggressive plan was in place. Under the shutdowns, Landry's was losing $1 million per day in revenue and had drawn $300 million of its existing credit line. So, the company invited investors to participate in a $250 million loan with an enticing 15% interest rate that would mature by October 2023. Fertitta also funnelled $50 million of his own money into the loan.

While all this was going on his Golden Nugget Online Gaming division (GNOG), business was booming, fuelled by people stuck at home gambling their federal stimulus money.

Having his business survived the pandemic lockdowns, Fertitta is now looking to build on the Las Vegas Strip. According to filings made by the Texas-based billionaire, there are plans to build a 43-story, 2,000-room hotel and casino on priorly purchased land—which initially cost $270m. Fertitta plans for the project to have multiple restaurants, a convention space, a wedding chapel, a 2,500-seater theatre and an auto showroom.

How it All Started

His father, Vic, owned a seafood restaurant on Galveston Island and after school, Tilman would peel shrimp in his father's restaurant. By age 14 he was managing the restaurant, learning the business hands-on.

In the late 1970s, after dropping out of the University of Houston, Fertitta started several business ventures, from a women's clothing shop, stores that sold vitamins, an arcade game distributor and a construction company. In 1985, at 28, he opened the 160-room Key Largo Hotel in Galveston. Soon he sold the Key Largo for $600,000 to his cousin Frank Fertitta (who, with brother Lorenzo, later became billionaires from casinos and mixed martial-arts promoter UFC, which they sold in 2016).

Tilman used that cash to help him buy Houston eateries Landry's Seafood Inn and Oyster Bar and Willie G's from the Landry brothers and expanded to Galveston, Corpus Christi and San Antonio. In the late 1980s, he started buying up restaurants on the marina boardwalk in Kemah, on Galveston Bay, turning 40 waterfront acres into his first "eatertainment" district, with Joe's Crab Shack, Saltgrass Steak House and more.

Tilman Buys a VVIP B767 for the Houston Rockets

In 2019, Fertitta purchased a Boeing B767 for his basketball team, Houston Rockets. It then spent much of nearly two years since to have it retrofitted for NBA needs. That includes video and meeting areas for coaches, card tables and seats ideal for sleeping. In April 2022, the players had their first flight from Houston to San Antonio, the attention was on the comfort.

Rockets players did not know they would be on the new charter until they boarded the plane.

"I mean, everything looks new," guard Eric Gordon said. *"It has a modern feel, a lot of TVs. You're not used to seeing big-screen TVs in there. It's definitely great, that's for sure."*

"It was sweet; it was so nice," Rockets coach Stephen Silas said. *"(Rockets owner) Tilman (Fertitta), man, wow. It was beautiful. There's the different sections, layback seats, everything was done to perfection. I'm very thankful to Tilman for doing that for us. It's definitely a perk."*

"I've been on six teams and I've never seen a plane like that one," Rockets centre Christian Wood said. "I know they took their time. You get on it and you're like, *'Wow man, so much space. It's so huge.' You're thankful for Pat (Fertitta) and Tilman spending their money to have that. We're going to have those longer flights soon, too."*

With all the airline disruption that is happening now after the lockdowns, with many airlines having scrapped certain routes, delays, cancelled flights. The Houston Rockets are going to have an advantage flying private on this amazing VVIP B767.

Quantum Economy Snippets

➢ Look at the purchase of a private jet, as an investment in your business.

Chapter 13
From High-School Drop-Out, to Entrepreneur, Fighter Jet Pilot, to Astronaut. Meet Jared Isaacman

Isaacman

"One of the best times at a start-up is when you've got the eight people in the basement eating Chinese food and everybody kind of shares knowledge and you share in your successes and failures together and you learn together."

—**Jared Isaacman**

Where It All Started

While in kindergarten Jared told his teacher he would go to space someday and she said she'd be watching. Growing up he knew that the odds of becoming a NASA astronaut were very slim, however this did not discourage him from hoping things would change one day.

As a ninth grader and a freshman Jared discovered that he and his best friend, Brendan Lauber, had a talent for fixing computers and started a computer repair business in his parents' basement called Deco Systems. He also worked at CompUSA in nearby Somerville, NJ. He had begun working, doing computer technical service and repair, when he was 14. Two years later, that work led him to an offer from one of his clients and he chose to drop out of high school to take the job, obtaining a GED along the way.

In 1999, Isaacman founded a retail payment processing company named United Bank Card, which was later renamed Harbour touch, a point-of-sale payment company based in Pennsylvania. By 2020, the company had been renamed Shift4 Payments.

Jared remained CEO and the company was processing US$200 billion in payments annually. Shift4 handles payments for a third of America's restaurants and hotels, including giants like Hilton, Four Seasons and KFC. Jared took it public in June 2020 and owns 38% of the stock.

Jared's Aviator Path Begins

Back in 2004, during the early days of his company; at just 21 years old, Jared was living in his parents' basement working around the clock, while burning himself out. He figured he needed to get a hobby, something to get him outside the office and that's when he decided to take his interest in aviation to something tangible.

Jared started flying Cessna 172s and once he got his private pilot's licence bought a Cessna Turbo 182 and after 150 hrs of flying, upgraded to a twin-engine Beechcraft Baron. He got his commercial, instrument and multi-engine ratings in the Baron. He flew that for about 700 hours over a year and a half and then moved onto jets.

When Did Jared Start Flying Private?

In 2005, he had never been on a private jet before because he never had the money. His motivation the first time he climbed on a private jet had nothing to do with business efficiency or time savings. He was purely driven by his enthusiasm for aviation. He discovered that it wasn't just cool but an efficient way to travel. Jared chartered a Lear 35 to go to Tucson, Arizona for a meeting. He soon figured why not buy a company jet and learn to fly it himself.

However, Jared is always about taking up new challenges and in 2008 made his first World Record attempt in a light jet; and missed the mark by just one hour after long ground holds in India and Japan. He didn't give up and on his second attempt shattered the record by over twenty-one hours, completing the route in sixty-one hours, fifty-one minutes.

By breaking the round-the-world velocity record in his Citation CJ2. Jared earnt an "experimental type" ranking allowing him to pilot L-39 Albatros and A-4 Skyhawk fighter jets, leading him into creating his own aerobatic squadron referred to as the Black Diamond Jet Team. Jared teamed-up with other 5 pilots and as a group flew over 100 air show exhibits between 2011 and 2014. They flew seven fighter jets, 18 inches apart, doing formation loops, rolls and other manoeuvres. The team included former USAF Thunderbirds and civilians like Jared.

Jared Starts a Private Air Force

Every time they sat down at the bar, the discussion turned to how they could not do the air show thing forever. At some point, they were going to have a bad day. They started brainstorming about how to pivot from something they enjoyed so much, to something that had real commercial opportunity but safer? The whole idea of "commercial adversaries" was born. It's not hard to believe that the government is very inefficient, they figured it will cost them more, than what they could do for less. They realised they could buy fighter jets from all over the world—A-4 Skyhawks right out of Top Gun, MiG-21s, F-16s—from New Zealand, the Czech Republic, Spain, Israel, etc. They could offer the government four or five planes in the air at one time for the same cost as what they would incur flying just one of their own F-16s. In 2012, Drakken International was born and by 2016, the business had grown to $6 billion. Drakken currently has close to 100 fighter jets and a high-margin, profitable business model. Jared sold part of his stake in Drakken in 2019, to Wall Street firm Blackstone for a nine-figure sum.

Next Step, Space

But Jared was aiming even higher and approached Elon Musk and in 2021 bought an entire passenger flight from SpaceX. He took three others with him on the world's first all-civilian spaceflight to orbit. The mission, called Inspiration4, raised more than $243 million for St Jude's Children's Research Hospital and is featured in the Netflix show, *Countdown: Inspiration4 Mission To Space.*

But he hasn't stopped at one space flight, his new adventure, the Polaris programme, was announced just recently, that will take Jared into space another three times. The first flight, called Polaris Dawn, will feature Commander Jared Isaacman, as the Mission Leader and three passengers, who will spend five days in orbit.

Next: Polaris Dawn, a new, five-day mission scheduled to blast-off later this year. The purpose of these next missions is to present how non-government astronauts may very well be productive in space. If Inspiration4 was profitable, they knew it might open the door to extra attention-grabbing missions. Now that the door is open, there's a lot to build and really open this frontier. Polaris is a sequence of technically demanding developmental missions that can conclude with the primary flight of the brand-new launch rocket, Starship that will lead back to the moon and the colonisation of Mars.

Polaris is a joint program with SpaceX, so they assembled two proficient engineers at SpaceX that they knew from Inspiration4: Sarah Gillis, the SpaceX lead astronaut coach and Anna Menon, a SpaceX managing engineer and mission director of mission management who beforehand worked as a biomedical operator at NASA. Jared added, Scott "Kidd" Poteet, who he flew with for over a decade in the Air Shows and at Drakken. Scott was also the mission director for Inspiration.

The next two missions after that will be Polaris II and III. Polaris IIs objective's will be based mostly on what will be learnt from Polaris Dawn and the un-crewed check flights of Starship. If profitable, Starship would be the spaceship that can return human beings to the moon and finally carry the primary people to Mars. Starship might sometime be the Boeing B737 of human spaceflight.

When Conquering Space Helps Your Business on Earth…

While Jared has been busy conquering space, Shift4 is expanding its reach on earth and to do that Jared has been flying his Global XRS back and forth from the US to Europe, allowing him to train for space while still building his business.

With all this media attention on Jared's space endeavours, his company Shift4 has taken the opportunity to branch out internationally. In March 2022 Shift4 (NYSE: FOUR), announced that it will acquire both Finara, a cross-border eCommerce payments provider with a large European presence and the Giving Block, which specialises in cryptocurrency fundraising for non-profits. These acquisitions better position the company to pursue a multi-trillion-dollar addressable market across the world, including accelerating growth in eCommerce, gaming, stadiums, restaurants, hospitality, specialty retail, charitable giving and a new capability with cryptocurrency enablement. Jared explains, *"Cryptocurrency is quickly moving beyond early adoption and becoming increasingly mainstream as more people want to invest, transact and donate in crypto."* They intend to be at the forefront of this movement and leverage The Giving Block technology across the entire Shift4 enterprise.

These two acquisitions are expected to contribute over $15B of end-to-end payment volume and $35M of adjusted EBITDA in 2023.

Success is About Learning to Handle Fear

When asked about success Jared says it is about learning how to handle fear. Jared explains, *"You compartmentalise, focus on what you can do not to get hurt or die. Right now, I'm training for a space mission [Polaris Dawn] six months from now. How I perform during that training and the knowledge I accumulate will help if I have a moment. I'll know what to do tactically. If you're flying an airplane and it stalls, it's going to hit the ground if you do nothing. So, you remove fear of hitting the ground from the equation, then do what you need to recover. Preparation is part of it, then compartmentalising, then doing everything tactically you can to mitigate a possible bad outcome. Also, I don't take unnecessary risks. A few of my air show buddies started riding motorcycles. I tried it for two days and I was like, 'I'm going to kill myself on this thing. It's not compatible with my skill set.' You have to know your limitations."*

I guess knowing your limitations and taking things one step at a time you can truly go to infinity and beyond.

Quantum Economy Snippets

- ➤ Keep asking challenging questions, this will lead to new ideas
- ➤ Aim high, you may even get into space.

Chapter 14
Even Plumbers Can Fly By Private Jet

"*Make decisions quickly and don't be afraid to make mistakes. As long as you are more right than wrong, you will win.*"

—Charlie Mullins

Charlie Mullins wasn't born into money. He's the son of a factory worker father and his mother worked as a cleaner. When he was born, they rented a couple of rooms in Camden, UK, before moving to the Rockingham Estate in London's Elephant and Castle.

At the tender age of ten, Charlie used to miss a few days of school to help Bill, his local plumber. As it turned out, Charlie was a natural in the trade and, having developed a talent for plumbing he left school aged 15 and gained City and Guilds qualifications to become an apprentice plumber.

Before long, Charlie had set-up shop as a sole trader in the Pimlico area of London, building a plumbing empire in London called Pimlico Plumbers, which, after forty years in business, he recently sold for over £145m ($170m) to American home services provider, Neighbourly.

The secrets to Charlie's success in building Pimlico Plumbers is a combination of common sense and out-of-the-box thinking—he makes it clear that obsessive focus on customers has been key, as has a determination to create a service that's professional and counter to the negative experiences many have of tradesman.

Among his common sense 'secrets' is, "We don't turn up late. We wear smart clothes and are transparent with our prices," he elaborates. "These aren't things people normally associate with plumbers."

On his out-of-the-box approach, Charlie spent £1m (USD $1.2m) on his 80 number plates which spell out plumbing-related themes, including 'Drains,' 'Sinks,' 'Shower,' 'Gas' and 'Loo 2 Rod.' But he says they are an investment in the business as he uses them on his vans. According to Charlie, they got noticed and have brought Pimlico Plumbers a lot of business as a result.

Introduced to Business Aviation

Charlie started using private jets a few years ago when he began investing in property in Marbella, Spain. He'd been negotiating a deal on a villa and someone else was closing in fast on the deal.

Needing to get from London to Spain to close the transaction before the other party did, the only solution, he recalls, was to fly private. That's how Charlie discovered the power of private jet travel. Ever since, he has shuttled between

London and Malaga on various chartered aircraft, often carrying guests.

Charlie first started chartering small Hawkers and Citation jets but has recently graduated to larger cabin aircraft, finding the extra space to be more comfortable and certainly worth the extra money.

According to him, the lockdowns have changed people's mindset towards air travel. "The hassle in airports, long lines at check-in, delays, last minute flight cancellations, diversions and lost baggage are all things people with the money can avoid by traveling by private jet," he says.

"Flying private, you control the schedule and you're guaranteed to get to your destination."

From Plumbing to the Music Industry

Since selling Pimlico Plumbers, Charlie has moved into the music business, where he has already spotted the talents of singer RaRa Lea. Charlie and Rachel (RaRa's real name) are spending a lot of time in Nashville getting her new album ready and preparing a US tour for later this year.

In fact, Charlie plans on spending quite a bit of time in the US, shuttling back to the UK and Spain and is currently either looking to buy some time on a jet or acquire his own, so that he can spring into action at a moment's notice.

Asked in a recent Biz Jet TV interview what advice he would give to a young person who loves the idea of having their own business and flying private, Charlie admitted that he is not a great fan of universities, believing people have to be more hands-on and get out there.

"Common sense, enthusiasm and different ideas," he shares. "You need to have a unique approach to what you do, have the guts to do things differently, while solving a problem."

"You always need to be in front of the queue," he adds. *"Make decisions quickly and don't be afraid to make mistakes. As long as you are more right than wrong, you will win."*

"In today's world, so many people are not very good at making decisions. Many people these days complicate business. You need to make it simple."

In his business, Charlie says they would turn up on time, do the job, clean up afterwards, all while providing a quality service. "People will always pay for quality and this leads back to private jets. Private jet travel does cost money but the quality is far higher than airline travel."

So, if a plumber from London can build a multi- million-dollar business repairing people's sinks and end up jetting around the world privately, how about you?

Quantum Economy Snippets

➢ Flying private gets you into deals faster than your competition, winning you more business.

- You need to have a unique approach to what you do, have the guts to do things differently, while solving a problem.

Chapter 15
Self-Development Gurus
Go Private Jet

"Success is the progressive realisation of a worthy goal or ideal."

—**Earl Nightingale**

Born from humble beginnings, the master of motivation, Tony Robbins has built an empire now with an estimated net worth of $480 million, according to Forbes. Robbins owns or is a partner in several companies, has written several best-selling books and provides life coaching to CEOs, political leaders and more.

I was exposed to Tony Robbins the first time back in 1991 when I was living in California and training to become a commercial pilot. I was struggling with flying multi-engine aircraft because of the speed. I started applying Tony Robbins' Neuro Associative Conditioning (NAC) by copying my Flight Instructor's physiology. My performance increased within the space of a few minutes. I completed my training successfully and went onto a successful career as a professional pilot.

But for all his advice on how to make lots of money, Robbins likes to spend money, too. Some of the things he buys are luxurious, some are not and some are for other people. Tony Robbins shared the one thing he buys to make his life easier or better:

"Private jets. Private flight. Extraordinary," he said. "There's nothing that changes quality of life when you travel as much as I do, as that." In fact, he was persuaded to give private flights a try after a 13-hour lost-luggage, delayed-flight ordeal between San Diego and Aspen, where he was visiting a billionaire friend for Christmas. Tony is a great believer in learning form successful people and when his billionaire friend told him how to bypass commercial flights, Tony tuned in.

Tony voiced his concern, as he was not a billionaire. His friend replied, "You didn't have to be a billionaire but needed to start thinking about how much time it would save him."

And he said, "Here's what you need to do. You need to go charter." He said, "Now if you go charter, you're not gonna like the price you see. 'Cause you're gonna see, 'I could've got a ticket for $800 and made all those trips. Now when I charter, this thing might cost me $5,000—for the small jet in those days—to do this trip.'"

He said, "But, I'm gonna tell you something, if you just take a budget and you just say, 'For the year I'm gonna spend this but I can go when I want, where I want, wherever I want, in the middle of the night, with my own food. I can sleep in the middle of the night 'cause I've got a bed on the plane.'"

He said, "It will change your productivity more than anything on earth." And it sounded insane. So he said, "Start with a small amount. Pick a number and just say you're gonna charter. Don't be stupid and buy a jet initially, start by chartering."

Tony Robbins started chartering and spending around $350,000 [per year] to charter small planes and was still taking commercial flights internationally because that was just too expensive for charter. He says that flying private changed his life. The value is unbelievable. Then in 2015 he sold one of his companies for a couple hundred million dollars. Traveling overseas so much, Robbins started looking at buying a Challenger or maybe a GIV but then he chartered one to go from Palm Beach to Poland for a private event and they had to stop in Newfoundland [to refuel and deal with a technical fault]. This made him think that if he was going to spend all that money, he needed to have a jet that could take him direct. The choice fell upon a pre-owned Bombardier Global XRS.

Robbins schedule is crazy at times but made a lot easier with the use of his Global XRS. In an in interview with *Business Jet Traveller Magazine* he told the story of a recent trip where he flew to Brazil to do an event in the Amazon, then from there to Toronto to do a seminar in front of 8,000 people. From there he flew to Las Vegas to be in front of 10,000 people. From Las Vegas to his resort in Fiji for two days and [without the jet] he said he wouldn't have gone at all because he would have not had the time. From there he went and did a 5,000-person, four-day event in Sydney, Australia and then flew straight to India, then from India back to London and then to the U.S. he circled the globe in 21 days. A couple of years ago he sold his Global XRS and bought a Boeing Business Jet, a flying apartment, allowing him to carry more people and have more room to relax while he travels around the world. Robbins stated that having his own jet has made him 10 times more productive.

10X Your Business with a Private Jet

Grant Cardone lost his father to a sudden heart attack when he was just 10. By his early teens he was into drugs and drinking. At 25 he was in a rehab centre, where he was told there was no hope for him and that he would never amount to anything. But Grant was ready to change...

He realised that if he wanted to be a successful entrepreneur, he needed to master the art of sales. He started working for a used car dealership, reading business and personal development books, attending seminars and applying what he learnt. As his car sales increased Grant started investing in real estate and build his wealth.

Today Grant is happily married to the woman of his dreams—Elena—and they have two daughters, Scarlett and Sabrina. He is the CEO of Cardone Enterprises and Cardone Capital, an international speaker, entrepreneur, author of New York Times bestseller 'The 10X Rule' and creator of 21 best-selling business programs. He also owns and operates seven privately held companies and a $5bn portfolio of multifamily properties.

Named the #1 marketer to watch by Forbes Magazine, Grant is also the founder of The 10X Movement and The 10X Growth Conference, the world's largest business and entrepreneur conference. What really distinguishes Grant from many other entrepreneurs is that he is unafraid to do things differently, to try something new, or think and act outside the box.

You can clearly see how he is the real deal by watching Discovery Channel's '*Undercover Billionaire.*' Grant says that starring on that show was the most difficult thing he's ever done. He was not allowed to use his real name, was only given a car and $100 and was delivered to Pueblo in New Mexico. Here in 90 days he took $100 and turned it into a business valued over $5.5m.

Cardone had become sick of being on the road +250 days a year delivering sales training all over the US, Canada and Mexico, with the occasional inter-continental gig. Over the last 10 years traveling through airports has become more and more time-consuming and troublesome. As he got married and started having children, he started using technology to reach his clients via video conferencing. He tried to avoid traveling as much as he could. Over the years Cardone had been building his real estate empire and saw that if he really wanted to expand exponentially air travel was necessary.

He spoke to billionaire friends, those that owned private jets advocated how much easier life was traveling this way, while other billionaire friends reckoned a private jet was stupid and a waste of money. Interestingly those against private aviation did not have their own jets.

Cardone weighed up chartering, fractional ownership and buying his own jet. Without ever having chartered a jet, in 2015 he went out and bought an 8 year-old preowned Gulfstream G200 for USD $8M. In his first year of operation Cardone's jet had flown 250 hours.

Cardone said his jet is like a holiday home, if you own one, you'll use it. However, a private jet depreciates so Cardone is always thinking of ways of using his jet to make him money. He doesn't charter it out to third party but keeps it exclusively available for his own use.

A typical day would see him fly to multiple locations, take his wife and kids with him and close a number of deals and back in time for dinner at home in Miami. The flexibility of going when he wants, flying into smaller airports closer to his meetings, adds tremendous edge to his business. Cardone also sends his jet out to pick clients up and says this certainly gets people's attention, increasing the odds of deals going through.

Cardone also likes the fact he has hired his own pilots and treats them like family. They know him and he knows them, no surprises. Cardone defines his private jet as a time machine and the single best investment he has ever made, in fact in his second year of biz jet ownership he credits the plane to being the key factor in doubling his business.

After two years of operating his Gulfstream G200 Grant found himself with a $50M tax bill. He decided to sell his jet and invest in a larger one, as a business expense, instead of giving the $50M to Uncle Sam. He bought a Gulfstream G550 and took his business on a series of world tours. Grant's wife and daughters joined him as he jetted from Miami to London, Dubai, Thailand, Australia, Fiji, Hawaii and back to Miami.

Towards the end of 2021 Grant kept getting calls from people wanting to buy his G550, so he took a good offer and went out and spent $60M on a Gulfstream G650ER. He doesn't look at how much it cost him to buy the jet, nor the hourly cost but he chooses to focus on the opportunities the jet opens up.

I met with Grant in January 2022 to do an interview for Biz Jet TV and he told me a very cool story. At the end of 2021, after numerous phone calls to a gentleman in Houston,

Grant was failing to get a meeting to do a large deal. One morning he woke up told his pilots to fire-up the G650 and flew to Houston. He rang the guy to tell him he just landed in Houston in his jet and was ready to meet with him, the guy accepted to see Grant and they did a $189M deal. Grant says that using his jet got him to close that deal and many others. You can only do so much over the phone and via zoom meetings, you get to a point where you need to meet face to face. Grant mentioned the having his own jet takes a lot of stress out of his life. He gets to his meetings relaxed and with all the energy and focus to put on his A-game and get deals done. Grant also recommends people to get themselves a bigger jet than they need. This just gets you to play in a higher league, close bigger deals and travel in comfort, with minimum stress.

Mini-Van in the Sky

Serial entrepreneur and New York Times bestselling author, Loral Langemeir has been flying private for over a decade and says her King-Air is like a Mini-van in the sky. She has been able to take her two kids with her on most business trips and found this invaluable as a single Mum. Loral advocates more business women should buy their own aircraft, as it allows better work-family balance.

Loral is based in Tahoe, Nevada and is involved in a number of ventures, from Real Estate in Boise, Idaho to growing medical Mariuana in Nevada and her auto dealership in Dallas. Loral also has a coaching business and is world renowned as the *Millionaire Maker*, as she helps people with building their wealth.

Loral also said that as a result of flying private, her son learnt to fly and as soon as he finishes college, wants his mum to buy a jet and he will learn to fly that too.

Quantum Economy Snippets

- Owning your own private jet improves your quality of life.
- No more lost luggage and no more flight delays.
- A hectic travel schedule can be made a lot easier by flying private.
- The private jet gives you more time to do the stuff you enjoy, like spending two days in Fiji…
- Traveling by airline got to become too much hassle and time consuming.
- Weighed-up chartering, fractional ownership and buying a jet. Chose buying a pre-owned jet because the commitment would cause him to fly more.
- Visit multiple locations in one day and take your family with you.
- Having your own jet reduces your stress.
- Don't be concerned with the price of the jet and the monthly running costs, focus on the opportunities it opens.
- Buy a bigger jet than you need. This graduates you to a higher league, leading to larger more lucrative deals.
- Take your family on business trips, let your jet become your minivan in the sky.

Chapter 16
Be Stupid, Buy a Jet:

A Lesson from a Billionaire

"'Be Stupid,' means doing anything reasonable people tell you not to do: be bold, be daring, push yourself to the limits, break the rules, follow your instinct and your heart, do something because you like doing it and don't worry when people warn you about the consequences."

—Renzo Rosso

Renzo Rosso is not a designer but he is in the fashion business. He is a marketing genius, a money-making machine in the most relaxed and fun way. Rosso is the creator of the Diesel fashion brand and author of the book, *"Be Stupid-For Successful Living."* Rosso explains how the braveness to make stupid decisions and the ability to see things for how they could be helped him build a successful company and become a billionaire. Buying his first private jet, a Learjet 45 was what many thought a stupid decision.

His CFO told him buying a jet was not a smart thing to do. Rosso, being the out of the box thinker he is, didn't listen. He bought the jet and used it as a business tool, flying him in and out of different cities with a speed the airlines couldn't, applying the philosophy of the future belonging to those who are fast. Once he saw his business growing exponentially, he ordered a brand new Dassault Falcon 7X, that gave him intercontinental range and took the Diesel brand global.

Just like Renzo Rosso's CFO told him that chartering or buying a private jet is not a good idea, yours will probably tell you the same. However, Clayton M. Christensen; Kim B. Clark Professor at Harvard Business School and a co-author of, "*Competing Against Luck: The Story of Innovation and Customer Choice*," said:

"Finance is taught independently in most business schools. Strategy is taught independently, too—as if strategy could be conceived and implemented without finance. The reality is that finance will eat strategy for breakfast any day—financial logic will overwhelm strategic imperatives—unless we can develop approaches and models that allow each discipline to bring its best attributes to cooperative investment decision making. As long as we continue this sliced approach to the MBA curriculum and experience, our leading business schools run the risk of falling farther and farther behind the needs of sectors our graduates aspire to lead."

Renzo Rosso didn't have an MBA and realised the private jet was his exponential time machine…running the numbers before buying a jet didn't show this but Rosso's vision did!

Quantum Economy Snippets

- Buying a jet early on in the business was completely against logic BUT the jet gave the time leverage necessary to grow the company in an accelerated 'fashion.'
- Innovation does not come from the balance sheet. Buying a private jet can sound and seem stupid BUT very often turns out to be a very smart choice!

Chapter 17
Combining Flying as a Hobby with Business

"To learn something but not to do is really not to learn. To know something but not to do is really not to know."
—Stephen R. Covey

Mark Leavitt helps run his family insurance business, the Leavitt Group out of the lovely town of Cedar City in Southern Utah.

The Leavitt Group was founded by Mark's father, Dixie back in 1952. Since then, the Leavitt Group has grown into one of the largest independent insurance brokers in the United States. Since 1989, consolidated revenues have climbed from $8 million to $191 million. Throughout this period of growth and success, agency profitability ratios have remained well above industry averages. Today the Leavitt Group has over 125 locations all across the US and is the 10th largest privately held insurance broker in the nation.

Mark grew-up with a passion for airplanes. When he returned from serving a two-year Mission for his Church in Bolivia, Mark's plan was to get his pilot's licence. He then got married and involved in the family business but eventually earning his wings in 1983 and bought a 1961 Cessna 182. In 1998 Mark started flying a Cessna C340 for business and Leavitt Group also bought a Beechcraft Kingair A100 and clocking-up over 700 hours a year. The Leavitt Group were one of the first companies to receive delivery of the Hondajet and they are putting it to work, flying their teams all over the US building their business.

In talking to Mark in one of our interviews on Biz Jet TV on YouTube, he explains how he uses his Hondajet to build the business. There are only two commercial flights a day out of Cedar City, which means if they had to fly commercial, they would have to drive over 2 1/2 hours to Las Vegas. Mark explained that it only takes him an hour flying to get to Durango, Colorado. This saves him stacks of time, as with the airlines between driving to the airport, TSA and all the rest of the hassle that comes with airline travel these days, this trip would take him 12 hours. Using the Hondajet to go and explore new business deals and being able to scramble to places for emergency meetings are two great benefits of owning your own jet.

Using private jets also allows Leavitt Group to be in Cedar City, Utah. With a population of just over 38,000 people and being a primarily Mormon town, there is also a very low crime rate. Over the past several years, Utah has made the list as one of the best places to live and start a business. In fact, according to the Gallup-Healthways Wellbeing Index, Utah is the #1 state to live in the future. Utah is home to five national parks and countless state and national monuments.

According to the Council for Community on Economic Research, Cedar City, almost across the board, has a lower

Dcost of living than many cities in the United States (85–90% lower than the US average cost of living) and most major cities within Utah.

If you like amazing outdoors, outstanding festivals, Cedar City offers a unique lifestyle. Being able to enjoy views of the red hills and alpine mountains every day and spectacular starry skies at night—not to mention crystal clear air every day of the year, are difficult to quantify on spreadsheets and data forms but they are a very real part of living in Cedar City.

Mark and his brothers enjoy living in Cedar City and the great lifestyle it offers, coupled with low cost of living has allowed them to attract and develop a great team at the Leavitt Group. So another great benefit of the private jet as a business tool is being able to locate your company where you like.

Quantum Economy Snippets

- ➢ If you like the idea of flying as a hobby, why not buy your own jet and fly it yourself. Let your business pay for your hobby.
- ➢ The private jet allows you to react immediately in cases of business emergency and get your team out very quickly and efficiently.
- ➢ Using private jets allows you to locate your business in a great place to live, the quality of life in your local area will allow you to attract and build a great team.

Chapter 18
How Have Covid Lockdowns Influenced the Future of Business Travel?

"Travel and change of place impart new vigour to the mind."
—**Seneca**

Since the pandemic first began, the drop in business travel has not only been affected by Covid-19 related restrictions. The reduction is also indirectly tied to corporate travel budgets, which were cut by nearly two-thirds at the peak of pandemic in 2020.

Further compounding the change, no economic crisis post the Second World War has lasted this long. Recovery is uncertain and according to a recent survey conducted by Roland Berger, 55% of respondents expect their post-crisis business travel to be at least 20% less than before.

Chubb, the world's largest publicly traded property and casualty insurance company, wanted to gauge perceptions about the impact of the pandemic on travel. What was lost during this period of severely limited travel? How did it impact the effectiveness of business travellers and their employers? In a remote working environment, with few or no opportunities to travel, what worked and what didn't?

The answers to these and other questions are important, as businesses make decisions about future travel budgets, return to office and the new criteria for traveling to meet with clients, develop business or attend conferences. What travel can be effectively replaced by meeting virtually? What is the opportunity cost of staying at your desk instead of getting on a plane?

This survey gives us insights into the views of business travellers across the world—in the United States, Europe, Asia Pacific and Latin America.

Among the key findings of the survey:

- Globally, 80% or more of business travellers believe they are missing something important when they cannot see body language or other visual clues that you can only get in an in-person meeting.
- Nearly three out of four business travellers (74%) say they are less effective in their job due to the pandemic and severely limited travel opportunities. Areas that have been negatively impacted include client service and the ability to maintain relationships with clients and business partners. With the proper precautions, respondents are twice as likely to feel more comfortable traveling for business than for leisure. One reason cited: business is important to their livelihood.
- A clear majority of business travellers (69%) expect that company travel budgets will be trimmed in a post-Covid world to reduce expenses.

- 75% of business travellers are willing to pay more to keep the middle seat open when they fly. 87% of business travellers have been personally concerned about contracting Covid during the pandemic and take steps to protect themselves, including wearing masks and social distancing. A smaller share (74%) say they always follow government rules. Another 24% say they sometimes follow Covid restrictions. Adherence to Covid safety protocols is highest among travellers in Latin America at 87%.

Since the start of the pandemic, more passengers have gravitated to private planes big and small for many reasons—like keeping ample distance from fellow travellers; or just getting to places where commercial airlines have stopped flying.

It's possible this will increase the use of jets by businesspeople and the growing number of millionaires and billionaires who love to travel and have plenty of money to do so in style and comfort of a private jet.

Although wealthy travellers are the ones demanding seats on private jets, it is private jet charter businesses that are actually buying the jets in significant numbers.

According to data collected by WINGX, business jets flew more sectors worldwide in 2021 than in any previous year on record. With 3.3 million flights from January through December, business jet traffic was 7% higher than in 2019, the previous high point for global business jet demand. Comparable growth was at its highest in the last month of the year, with the month of December seeing 23% more sectors flown than December two years ago. Over the holiday period

(December 20th—Jan 2nd), business jets flew 127,000 sectors, 41% more than in the same period two years ago. In contrast, scheduled airline passenger traffic was down by 28% versus December 2019, in line with the full year trend. Cargo operations showed similar resilience to business jets during 2021, with dedicated cargo sectors up 8% compared to 2019.

Private jet sales inventory is half what it usually is, hovering around 5% of the worldwide fleet. We are witnessing an increase in people that before were charter customers or had a share in a jet fractional ownership program, now moving into full ownership. Having your own jet, you control, offers you more flexibility and the certainty you can spring into action at any given time. While zoom video conferencing allows you to get a lot of work done remotely, you get to a point where the quickest and most effective way to get a deal done is a face-to-face meeting.

Kenn Ricci, the CEO of fractional jet ownership company, Flexjet, recently told Bloomberg Media that business is now so good that he plans to expand his fleet by 40% over the next year. And the recent success of private aviation has led the demand for new aircraft to drastically outpace supply, Bloomberg reported. "It's a once-in-a-lifetime grab," Ricci said. Ricci isn't alone in being optimistic about business aviation's future, Warren Buffet's Netjets is increasing their fleet by 30%. VistaJet, a unit of Dubai-based Vista Global Holding, also announced expansion plans, with plans to add a billion dollars in new private jets over the next 24 months. It said the move reflects increased demand from corporate executives. The additional aircraft are all from Bombardier. Plans call for accepting a dozen ultra-long-haul

Global 7500s, plus a new order for 10 super-midsize Challenger 350s.

I think the pandemic has accelerated the development of a lot of technology, allowing us to work remotely and making us realise that you don't always have to launch on a four-day trek to the other side of the world for a meeting, when it can be done via video conferencing or done with Virtual Reality. I see business travel decreasing but more people moving from Business and First-Class travel into flying private.

The question is, are you going to have a private jet in your business tool kit that will put you ahead of your competition?

Quantum Economy Snippets

- Business travel to be at least 20% less than before.
- 80% or more of business travellers say they are missing important visual clues that you can only get in an in-person meeting.
- Business jets flew 127,000 sectors, 41% more than in the same period pre pandemic.

Chapter 19
Maybe It's Time to Get a Custom Fit Private Jet

"The best investment I've ever made was in myself, the second best was in my private jet."

—Grant Cardone

Most people that decide to buy a private jet either ask someone they know and/or turn to the internet. This is not like buying a house, a car or a yacht, planes go up into the sky and last thing you want is something going wrong.

When you start navigating the internet looking for a jet you will invariably land on websites where you'll see lots of different jets for sale. What you need to realise is the people advertising the jets are either owners or most of the times brokers representing owners. You will phone them up and they will send you pretty pictures and maybe a video of the jet and tell you it is the most wonderful aircraft in the world and the price is a steal of a deal. Bear in mind these people represent the owner, not you.

My advice is to hire an aviation advisor/consultant, that represent you. This person will be able to help you select the right jet for your needs, be knowledgeable about the market and also help you with management once you take delivery. The process of buying a jet is quite technical and you need to get it right. Always remember: "*You are not buying a jet, you are buying time.*"

Whether you buy a new jet or pre-owned very often depends on your tax jurisdiction and if you can write-off the aircraft depreciation. Some people think a ten or twenty-year-old jet is dangerous but that is a myth. It all depends on how the plane has been maintained and flown. Today you can buy an older jet and have the interior custom-fit with all the latest technology and even wrap the jet in your company colours.

One of my companies, custom-fits jets for people. We will sit down with you in one of our showrooms or in our Virtual Showroom, in the comfort of your home and first understand your travel needs, your business, brand and style. From here we will recommend a particular jet. Our job will then to be to talk to every owner in the world that owns one of those jets and find the right one for you to buy. We can then change the interior, upgrade the cockpit, put winglets on it or whatever can and wants to be done.

There is only so much information I can give you in this book or on Biz Jet TV, it will always be general information and not specific or custom-fit to you.

To use a golf analogy: you can see someone on YouTube talk about his amazing new Callaway driver and decide to buy one. You purchase online, you start playing with it and do quite well. Someone else would have seen the same video and seek the advice of a professional golf club custom-fitter. Maybe the Callaway driver is right for you but you would benefit from a different shaft or a different driver all together.

Once you get custom fit you will have the best clubs for you, for the stage you're in of the game. You need to think about private jet acquisition in the same way. To make that quantum leap, you need to make a quantum decision and not linear. Undercover Billionaire star, entrepreneur and owner of a Gulfstream G650ER; Grant Cardone, suggests getting a bigger jet than you actually need because it can go further and will get you to stretch and grow your business 10X, in a quantum fashion, not linear.

Quantum Economy Snippets

- ➢ Consult with an aviation advisor.
- ➢ Get a custom-fit solution.
- ➢ Get a bigger jet than you need.

Chapter 20
The eVTOL Buzz

"The scientists of today think deeply instead of clearly. One must be sane to think clearly but one can think deeply and be quite insane. Be alone, that is the secret of invention; be alone, that is when ideas are born. The present is theirs; the future, for which I really worked, is mine."

—Nikola Tesla

There is a lot of talk about the environment and electric aircraft; one subject I have written about quite often in AvBuyer Magazine and also talked about on episodes of Biz Jet TV, is the world of eVTOLs (**e**lectric **V**ertical **T**ake-**O**ff and **L**anding). At time of writing there are close to 500 of these projects being worked on worldwide and lots of hype and money being thrown at this sector. There is no doubt that this technology is on its way.

However, there are many hurdles these eVTOL projects need to overcome, before they can be certified to fly commercially. *Personally, I see many similarities when it comes to eVTOL development with the Very Light Jet (VLJ) craze at the start of the millennium. Like the VLJ market, most of the companies developing eVTOL projects have never designed, built, tested, certified, produced and supported an aircraft.*

Combine this with their lack of information on prices, operating costs and inability to show a real business case, could we be set to witness several more financial disasters? After all, the VLJ buzz had a failure rate of 95%, with just the Hondajet and Embraer Phenom 100 surviving, joined later by the Cirrus VisionJet.

There are many applications for eVTOL aircraft, whether solving the 'last mile' or 'door-to-door' challenge by moving people quickly; from a company office to meetings in city centres' that are near existing heliports or newly constructed vertiports, or to outlying airports so passengers can depart on a business jet or scheduled airline flight.

An eVTOL is a lot cheaper and more efficient than a helicopter. I could see UHNWIs having one of these eVTOLs parked in a hangar next door to the house and using it to fly to the local airport, perhaps jumping into their Gulfstream G800 or Falcon 10X and flying to the other side of the world.

Urban areas will need the right infrastructure in place to serve the eVTOLs. Starting with existing heliports, as they have the operating certificates and air rights to begin stationing eVTOL aircraft immediately. Some heliports would need to undergo modification to offer recharging stations, hybrid vehicle refuelling facilities, passenger shelters and other amenities.

However, the cost to retrofit a simple landing pad into an eVTOL vertiport would be very affordable. Heliports currently in use will likely see the addition of and transition to eVTOL aircraft and those heliports not in use—a goldmine in economic opportunity sitting idle—will obtain revised operating certificates and air rights for Urban Air Mobility (UAM) use.

And, with airlines such as United, Virgin and American Airlines already having ordered fleets of eVTOLs, various airports will seek to blend UAM with conventional airport operations to maximise the utility and convenience of its facilities. Airports are the logical point of entry for eVTOLs into an urban transportation network.

Another great area for eVTOLs to help businesses is in cargo transport. Areas of the world with little infrastructure, like Africa or the islands of Indonesia, will benefit from this. It will allow them to move freight a lot quicker and at a fraction of the cost of flying by helicopter. This no doubt will result in lifting economies in remote locations and help businesses prosper.

There will be a few growing pains along the way but these new flying machines will change the way we travel short distances. Overall, eVTOLs will increase our speed, lower our transportation costs and simultaneously keep the air clean.

Quantum Economy Snippets

- eVTOL technology can take you from your home to your jet.
- eVTOL technology is cleaner.
- Most eVTOL projects will fail, like the VLJs did.
- It is predicted that 25 eVTOL project will get to market.

Chapter 21
Wrapping-Up to Speeding-Up

"Speed is often confused with insight. When I start running earlier than the others, I appear faster."
—**Johan Cruyff**

By now you have realised that a biz jet really does…buy you time, moves you faster, as well as keeping you safer and comfortable, reduces stress, gives you access to larger more lucrative deals, allowing you to live where you really want to.

A biz jet should never be looked at taking into the account the balance sheet cost but by the number of new opportunities it offers. These new business deals would not be possible without private jet travel…

I could not finish this book without talking about one of my favourite subjects in aviation, supersonic and hypersonic flight.

As we have talked about so far, everything has and is accelerating around us, exponential change is happening across many different business sectors. However, since Concorde's retirement, aircraft are moving at the same speed as back in the 1950s. In the world of smart phones, the internet, AI and lots more to come the world needs to fly faster.

A handful of companies such as Spike Aerospace, Boom Aerospace, Gulfstream and Dassault are all competing to bring to market the first Supersonic Business Jet (SSBJ).

One of the things that has slowed the development of this technology is the restriction of civilian supersonic flight over the continental United States. President Donald Trump actually started to pass new laws that, if not changed, will lead to supersonic flights being allowed over continental US.

Boom Aerospace claims its jet will fly from New York to London in just three hours and 15 minutes, basically halving the time it takes conventional airliners and private jets. With Virgin boss Richard Branson already having optioned to buy 10 of the supersonic Boom jets and a prototype being currently built, this project is leading the supersonic quest.

Like everything mentioned in this book, the first to market will win the race.

On the other spectrum of speed is Hermeus, an Atlanta-based start-up whose goal is to develop hypersonic aircraft. It's already testing a new type of engine it says will eventually be capable of reaching Mach 5 (over 3,000 mph). The engine is designed for a small, unmanned hypersonic aircraft Hermeus is currently creating for the US Air Force but scaled to a bigger size, it will be able to power a passenger plane. Hermeus hopes to get it in the air for the first test flight before the decade is out, in 2029—but because its technology has to be built almost entirely from the ground up, the company is already planning it out. For a start, it will be much smaller than current airliners and even Concorde, which had a capacity of around 100 passengers.

Science fiction writer Ben Bova in his novel, 'Moonrise' talks about Clipperships, which are rockets flying people from anywhere to anywhere on earth in less than an hour.

In the 1990s Pete Conrad, Apollo 12 astronaut who walked on the Moon in 1969, worked at McDonnell Douglas to develop the Delta Clipper-X. This was a reusable rocket shuttle that would take off and land vertically. But McDonnell Douglas abandoned the Clipper-X and Conrad's attempt to start his own passenger rocketry company, Universal Space Lines, went nowhere.

This however could become reality soon. SpaceX CEO Elon Musk said, during his keynote speech in 2017 meeting of the International Astronautical Congress in Adelaide, Australia, *"If you build a ship that's capable of going to Mars, what if you take that same ship and go from one place to another on Earth?"*

His answer: City-to-city rocket service, the fastest commercial transit ever created. Basic ballistic physics yields some amazing travel times. Los Angeles to Tokyo would take 32 minutes. A trip from New York to Los Angeles, which currently takes between 5 and 6 hours, would be reduced to 25 minutes. The 15-hour flight from New York to Shanghai would take just 39 minutes.

We just witnessed Star Trek actor William Shatner prove that even a 90-year-old can travel on a rocket, during his 10-minute ride to space on Jeff Bezos' Blue Origin reusable rocket. While this did take-off and land in Texas, it could have easily landed in Australia with a few more minutes' flight…

SpaceX released an animation showing the rockets leaving from and arriving on, offshore platforms just outside of each city. Musk, meanwhile, said that trips to Mars would carry about 100 people. However, he also said that his rocket cabin had the capacity of an Airbus A380, which can hold more than 850 passengers.

For those of you thinking that using rockets for long-haul travel would be expensive, that is true if the rocket is used only once. But, because of the reusability of today's rockets the cost has dropped—and by carrying 850 passengers, the cost per seat will be close to a First-Class ticket on an A380.

I have no doubt that by 2030 we will see supersonic flight, hypersonic flights and maybe even Clipperships, flying people on rockets. In the meantime, if you want to be ahead and take advantage of the amazing new opportunities arising throughout the world because of emerging markets, demographics, technology, Artificial Intelligence (AI) and lots more…there is only one way to travel…bringing you into the quantum economy!

Quantum Economy Snippets

- A biz jet should never be looked at taking into the account the balance sheet cost but by the number of new opportunities it offers.
- Supersonic or Hypersonic business jet travel is coming soon.
- Elon Musk will be flying people on rockets from anywhere on the planet to anywhere on the planet in less than an hour.
- Are you going to join the Quantum Economy?